ANXIOUS ATTACHMENT RECOVERY

OVERCOME INSECURITY &
FEAR OF ABANDONMENT BY
HEALING YOUR INNER CHILD
TO BUILD SECURE, LOVING &
LASTING RELATIONSHIPS

EMILY JOHNSON

© **Copyright 2024 - All rights reserved.**

The content contained within this book may not be reproduced, duplicated or transmitted without direct written permission from the author or the publisher.

Under no circumstances will any blame or legal responsibility be held against the publisher, or author, for any damages, reparation, or monetary loss due to the information contained within this book, either directly or indirectly.

Legal Notice:

This book is copyright protected. It is only for personal use. You cannot amend, distribute, sell, use, quote or paraphrase any part, or the content within this book, without the consent of the author or publisher.

Disclaimer Notice:

Please note the information contained within this document is for educational purposes only. All effort has been executed to present accurate, up to date, reliable, complete information. No warranties of any kind are declared or implied. Readers acknowledge that the author is not engaged in the rendering of legal, financial, medical or professional advice. The content within this book has been derived from various sources. Please consult a licensed professional before attempting any techniques outlined in this book.

By reading this document, the reader agrees that under no circumstances is the author responsible for any losses, direct or indirect, that are incurred as a result of the use of the information contained within this document, including, but not limited to, errors, omissions, or inaccuracies.

CONTENTS

INTRODUCTION V

Chapter 1. Understanding Attachment Styles 1
Exploring Attachment Theory. 2
Different Attachment Styles 6

Chapter 2. Understanding Anxious Attachment 15
Origins of Anxious Attachment 20
Unraveling the Emotional Web. 26
Fear of Abandonment 28

Chapter 3. The Impact of Anxious Attachment on
Everyday Life 31
Self-Esteem and Self-Worth 36
Identifying Anxious Attachments 39
Understanding the Fear of Abandonment. 41

Chapter 4. Anxious Attachments in Romantic
Relationships. 45
Patterns of Love. 46
The Struggles for Love. .52
The Fear of Abandonment. 55

Chapter 5. Overcoming Anxious Attachment 61

Addressing Anxious Attachments 63

Healing Past Wounds 74

Breaking the Cycle. 77

Chapter 6. Building a Better Self 81

Empowering Self-Discovery 82

Developing Self-Awareness 89

Building Healthy Boundaries 94

Chapter 7. Embracing Secure Attachment 101

Tools for Nurturing Secure Attachments. 105

Tools for Transformation 108

Chapter 8. Ending With Success .115

Finding Your Own Success 118

CONCLUSION 121

THANK YOU 127

REFERENCES 129

INTRODUCTION

One basic human trait that makes us intricately more complex than any other species on this planet is that we are beings who thrive on social interactions. We are designed to form meaningful relationships and live lives that are foundationally based on social elements.

From the moment we are born, we have an innate inclination to form bonds with other people. In fact, this need is so deeply rooted in our minds that the first relationship we ever form is a strong and unwavering connection with our mothers. This primary and foundational relationship that we have with our mothers is of such great importance that it will seep into all the facets of our lives later on, even as we grow into adults.

When you consider the magnitude and long-lasting effects that our primary relationships can have on us, it becomes glaringly obvious how important it is for us to not only have sturdy attachments but also have healthy attachments with the figures who will ultimately form the cornerstones of our relationship bonds.

While these relationships are paramount and form the blueprint of how we will develop relationships later on in life, in some unfortunate cases, the foundation that is formed is a negative one. Many people find themselves having trouble in their relationships as adults, and upon further investigation, they realize that they have formed what has become known as anxious attachment styles.

Anxious attachment styles are usually categorized by having difficulties in relationships that are dominated by strong feelings of insecurity and an unhealthy attachment to one's partner or the person with whom they have a relationship. It is also categorized as being afraid of deep and intense emotion or intimacy, a disregard for other people's feelings and emotions, excessive neediness, a desperate need for intimacy but an inability to trust others, and being anxious, jealous, and insecure when you are away from your partner *(Brennan, 2021)*.

With these anxious attachments being formed in childhood, they have a tendency to follow people into their adulthood, which ultimately affects the friendships and relationships they form with other people. And since we are inherently social beings, this attachment style can be detrimental to the success of our relationships and friendships.

If you, dear reader, have picked up this book, chances are that you have found yourself in relationships that seem wanting, unfulfilling, and like there is an uneven weightedness that seems to pull you down in the relationship.

My name is Emily Johnson, and I am a relationship counselor who has helped countless clients overcome the relationship challenges that many face but that not many know they are facing. Life is too short for us to have relationships that are anything other than fulfilling. In a world that forces you to work hard and push harder, your relationship needs to be your comfort, a soft place for you to land after you have faced the day's difficulties. In my years as a couple's therapist, I have helped people grow and nourish their relationships into the most fulfilling bond they can cultivate. But my focus has gone far beyond that work: I have also worked with individuals who have gone through break-ups and divorces, I have helped them cope with the unique loss of a relationship and partner, and I have helped them heal from within, preparing them for the next phase of life, whether or not that phase involves another relationship.

I started my writing journey as a way to share my experiences and knowledge with more individuals and couples. I hope to help my readers overcome the very same challenges my clients have faced.

While many people are not eager to admit that they are facing challenges in their relationship, the first step is acknowledging that there is something you are not entirely satisfied with. Then you can put in the work toward remedying the situation. Perhaps you are going through relationship troubles that are hard to pinpoint, feel insecure in your relationship, or feel like you depend too greatly on your partner. In this book, we are going to venture down the path of learning and self-healing.

In this book, you will learn

- how to identify anxious attachment styles in your life.
- how these anxious attachment styles can impact your relationships and your daily life.
- how to identify and categorize the different attachment styles that form.
- how to become more secure and confident, not only in your relationships but in your life in general.
- how to set firm and unwavering boundaries with others.
- how to overcome the anxious attachments that exist in your relationship through detailed and actionable steps that will allow you to experience healthy, happy, and fulfilling bonds.

An anxious attachment style is quite complex in terms of how it forms and develops. It stems from deep parental inconsistencies that cause a child to learn behaviors and attachments that affect them later on in life. A child who has a parent who is always there for them, supports them, gives them attention, and gives them the love and affection they so deeply desire is more likely to develop secure attachment later in life and will have the ability to form healthy bonds in every relationship they have.

However, anxious attachment styles develop as soon as there is an inconsistency in the parent-child relationship. In many cases, anxious attachment forms when a parent is attentive to a child's needs sometimes, and then other times, they are unavailable, not attuned, or unaware of their child's needs. The child experiences that their need is unmet, and as they grow older, they grow cautious of people who may also fail to meet their needs. The child grows into an anxious, insecure adult who fears being abandoned and is always looking out for a threat, even when none exists *(The Attachment Project, n.d.)*.

Allow me to share two instances that I experienced with clients. The first was a woman who had an anxious attachment style in all of her romantic relationships. After a string of failed relationships, she had finally found "the one." She had found the man she was going to spend the rest of her life with, but it didn't come without its challenges. In this relationship, as with all her other failed relationships, my client would become hypervigilant, which was further driven by her fear of abandonment. She would be consistently insecure and always question her partner about whether or not he was unfaithful. Despite him constantly proving to her that he was indeed faithful, it became taxing on their relationship, which ultimately led to her coming in to see me. The cause of her insecure attachment arose from her father leaving her and her mother when she was six years old and remarrying shortly after. This difficult situation left my client with a strong and deep fear of abandonment and a constant need to be reassured that her partner loves her.

I had another client who constantly found himself returning to an abusive relationship. He had a partner who would lie to him, be unfaithful, and hurl insults and emotional abuse at him. However, he constantly found himself going back, despite knowing how bad this relationship was for his mental and emotional health. You see, anxious attachments usually cause people to return to abusive relationships because although those with anxious attachments are unable to fully trust others, they depend on others to fulfill their emotional needs, making them codependent on the one person to whom they have grown comfortable with, no matter how disruptive and abusive the relationship may be *(Manson, 2021)*. There is also a deep inclination for those who have insecure attachment styles to make irrational and deeply emotional decisions which is often what caused my client to return to his harmful relationship time and time again, despite it being detrimental to his well-being and his being logically and consciously aware of the harm it was causing him—his emotions led his decisions.

But both of these cases had a positive outcome where, by working on themselves and overcoming their attachment issues, both clients were able to form and develop healthy and fulfilling relationships. They were also made aware of what caused them trauma in their early childhood, and they were able to actively avoid making the same mistakes with their own kids.

Despite how anxious or insecure you may feel in your relationship or even in your day-to-day life, this anxiousness can be overcome. There is an opportunity available to you to live confidently and happily. Let us go on this unique journey of learning how to overcome anxious attachments and how to be independent in your relationships. There is a promise of hope and fulfillment in your relationships that will come from the ultimate success of overcoming your anxious attachments.

So let us choose healing, and let us heal together!

CHAPTER 1

UNDERSTANDING ATTACHMENT STYLES

If a deep dissatisfaction has bubbled up within you about your relationships and about the way you have formed connections, you may have haphazardly scoured the internet to figure out what the problem is. Let me tell you that recognizing the deep dissatisfaction that exists is already a major step toward your full and complete healing.

It is all too easy for us to fall into a lull or a sense of complacency, getting comfortable with the things that hurt us because the thought of change seems slightly more intimidating. Instead, in this chapter, we are going to take a deeper dive into the different attachment styles that exist, which one you may be experiencing, and the effects it may have on your life and relationships. We will further look at the emotional issues that may arise, and through case-based examples, I will show you ways in which you can objectively understand your attachment style without driving yourself deeper into a pit of judgment and despair.

Exploring Attachment Theory

Deeply rooted in the psychological need for us to form bonds, attachment theory found its place in social studies. Attachment theory looks closely at the bonds and relationships we form with people on a long-term basis. It pays close attention to the bonds we establish with our caregivers from the moment we are born, and it looks at the romantic and life-long relationships we are bound to form later in life as well, whether it is relationships with people in our families, our friends, or our romantic partners.

However, attachment theory does not stop here. It doesn't end just by looking at each of these individual bonds that we have at different times in our lives. It delves much deeper than that, looking at how each relationship impacts and influences other relationships that are still to come. From subtle nuances to deep trauma, attachment theory looks at how, why, and when we form different relationships.

One way to think about attachment theory is that every relationship that we have in our life span is purposeful, and we intentionally develop bonds with specific people whether the reasoning behind our intentions is conscious or not. In the deep recesses of our minds and hearts, we seek fulfillment in specific ways from specific people, which further shapes the attachment styles that we develop.

Let us consider the following example: If a child is often left alone by their mother for any reason, they may face feelings of abandonment. They may feel that since they were always left to fend for themselves, they deserve this type of relationship, and they actively seek out similar relationships. In contrast, they may feel like they were severely abandoned and alone, and they actively seek out relationships that entirely eliminate the possibility of them experiencing the same loneliness once again. These subtle attachments that were formed in this person's life as a child affected the type of bonds, attachments, and relationships they developed when they were older, whether they were aware of it or not.

While some people may suggest that their early childhood has been dealt with, that they have overcome trauma, or that they have no influence from childhood on their adult life, these statements are entirely untrue. Something as small as food preferences, social preferences, emotional acclimation, and one's belief system are all established from a very young age, and people either pursue or lean into these aspects of life that have molded them, or they steer clear of it as a way of avoiding it entirely. Whichever direction they steer in, the influence is there.

Delving even further into attachment theory, we can see that there are different stages of attachment that follow individuals from this important developmental stage as an infant all the way to adulthood. The four stages are as follows *(Cherry, 2023)*:

1. **Pre-attachment stage:** From birth to six weeks of age, all infants depend on a caregiver to meet their basic

needs for food and warmth. Most infants will become accustomed to a specific caregiver at a certain age. However, during this infancy age, before the age of six weeks, the baby doesn't show any form of attachment to one individual person. Now, while studies do show that babies after the age of about two months tend to show a preference for their mothers, newborns accept comfort from anyone, hence this stage being the pre-attachment age.

2. **Indiscriminate attachment stage:** Between the ages of six weeks to seven months old, infants begin recognizing the different roles of the people in their vicinity. It is at this age that their attachments slowly begin forming and where they begin categorizing primary and secondary caregivers.

3. **Discriminate attachment stage:** From seven months to ten months, children begin openly expressing an attachment, bond, and preference for one parent over the other, or over anyone else, for that matter. It is usually at this age that they will begin showing a preference toward the mother as their primary caregiver because of the time that a child spends with their mother and the type of care a mother provides her child with.

4. **Multiple attachment stage:** Finally, from ten months onward, children tend to grow the bonds and attachments that they have with everyone in their lives, from the primary and secondary caregivers to grandparents and even extended family members.

Because our attachments are established at such a young age, that is where the focus is given when adults face difficulties or challenges in their attachments and relationships. Most people will look back on their childhood and how attachments were formed to pinpoint why certain relationship challenges may arise in their adulthood. Even I, when working with clients, find it most effective to start at the beginning and to look at and assess the type of attachments that were formed in early childhood as a means of understanding the relationships they currently have.

I find that in most cases, an individual may not even remember some of the aspects of their childhood or early development that had a great impact on their attachment styles. This work usually involves digging deep and trying to uncover what their minds would rather forget.

In fact, the study of attachments from infancy has been so profound and has played such a major role in psychology that even the likes of Freud had been specific not to avoid these bonds and attachments during development. John Bowlby was considered the first-ever attachment theorist when he developed the notion of attachment as the unseen and intangible connections between human beings that exist on a psychological level, encompassing our emotions and other elements of psychology.

However, attachment is not quite as straightforward as picking a caregiver and sticking to them for all one's primary needs. When you consider that the type of attachments we form with our caregivers will impact our future relationships, it is clear that the importance of these attachments needs to be appropriately considered. Because we have the innate need and ability to form close bonds with caregivers from an extremely young age, and because these relationships impact our future relationships, it means that it is both a learned and innate capability, adding further to the complexity of attachments.

Different Attachment Styles

Each person is unique, as are the bonds and attachments they develop with their caregivers and others. While each of us forms different connections with others, professionals have devised four general attachment styles into which most people can be categorized. As parents are growing more and more aware of the way in which they raise their kids, employing conscious parenting methods to form healthy attachments in their adulthood, attachment theory has become the focus of many new parents or soon-to-be parents. After all, at the basis of every parenting relationship is the notion that none of us want to raise scorned or emotionally traumatized kids.

Parents are fully aware that they will shape the way their kids interact with the world and with other people, so they have become attuned and more educated on the different forms of attachment styles so that they can raise their kids to form the best and healthiest attachments as adults.

Let us take a closer look at the four different attachment styles that exist *(Lewis, 2020)*:

1. **Secure attachment:** In a perfect world, every parent desires to form bonds with their children that are healthy and fulfilling. The secure attachment style is what every parent is hoping for. In this attachment style, parents prove time and time again to be there for their kids. They show their kids that even when the child leaves, the parent will be there for them when they return. With a parent who proves that they are always there for their child, who nurtures and protects them, and who corrects their wrongdoings in a kind and loving way, children tend to grow up with a sense of trust, good self-esteem, the ability to be in touch with their emotions, a trusting nature, and the capability to form successful relationships. When you develop a secure attachment with your child, you are present, sensitive to their emotions, responsive to their needs, and accepting of all emotions they express.

2. **Anxious-insecure attachment:** Children thrive on routine and predictability, especially when you consider that they don't have much control of even their own bodies. Knowing what can be expected makes them feel safe and secure. However, when they experience an inconsistent presence and support from their parents, they don't have the study ground on which trust is built. In the anxious-insecure attachment style, parents are often found to respond to their children's needs in a sporadic

and inconsistent way. They might be there sometimes, but other times are unavailable. This unpredictability usually leads to children not wanting to separate from their parents in case their parent leaves; it leaves them to be untrusting and they become extremely clingy to quite an exaggerated extent. This outcome stems almost entirely from inconsistency on the parent's part, leaving the child without a firm or secure sense of trust.

3. **Avoidant-insecure attachment:** There are instances when parents are unable to respond to their child's needs with sensitivity and patience. This response leads to the child shutting their parent out when they are in need or when they face an emotionally distressing situation because past experiences show that their parent won't be helpful. In most cases, the parent may diminish the feelings of the child when they are in distress, not meet the child's needs or demands, and not be helpful even in the moments when the child is clearly struggling with a difficult task. These choices should not be confused with encouraging independence as the parent's behavior is erratic and requires the child to assist them instead of them assisting their child. This behavior leads to the child logically drawing a conclusion that avoidance is the best route to take when dealing with their parent. They may also suppress their own emotions under the realization that even if they do express their emotions, their parent won't respond.

4. **Disorganized-insecure attachment:** In cases where children are raised with this attachment type, it is often

seen that the parents themselves suffered some form of unresolved trauma as a child. They respond in ways that are not entirely normal for a caregiver. They tend to engage with their child in harsh ways, they scare their child intentionally or unintentionally, and they ridicule and reject their child's emotions. Because of these consistent negative interactions with parents, the child usually shows aggression toward the parent and later toward others; they reject help, assistance, or care from the parent when it is offered, and they force themselves to become self-reliant.

The complexities that arise from these attachments are that parents don't only fulfill the role of caregiver, but the remnants of the bonds that we formed with our children will be left in their lives forever. Long after they have left the proverbial nest and after they have begun building lives of their own, they will find someone who will become their closest bond. The way their bond with us was formed will be mirrored in every relationship they have in the future.

Having established the different types of attachment that exist between the parent and the child, it still may be too far removed from reality based on the theoretical approach listed above. Instead, to see what is mirrored and experienced in our own lives, we need to understand what these attachment styles look like in real life. Below, I am going to share specific case studies that I have handled with several clients.

Secure Attachment

I once had a client who was extremely confident in her feelings. She was well-adapted and emotionally well-regulated. When I say that she was confident in her feelings, I mean that she confidently expressed the complex range of emotions that human beings are expected to face. This process means that when she was afraid or nervous, she would openly communicate those feelings with confidence. This client had an open and secure attachment with her parents and endeavored to do the same with her own kids. This behavior meant that after a day at school, her kids would openly communicate about when they felt shy, nervous, or scared at school. They were so confident in the relationship and bond that they had with their mother that they were willing to discuss strong feelings that bothered them long after the feeling had passed. They were also far more empathetic with other children who also expressed fear, always leaping at an opportunity to comfort their peers.

Her kids never spent a moment waiting to be comforted or soothed by her, and she was raised with the notion that loving and caring for your child and giving them attention and affection was not spoiling them. In turn, she watched her children learn to process and express their emotions in healthy ways no matter how big their emotions were.

Anxious-Insecure Attachment

There are many people that I have encountered who generally just come across as anxious. They seem to be more on edge than other people, more distrusting, and less inclined to come out of their shells when engaging or interacting either with me or with other people. This behavior can often stem from anxious-insecure attachment.

I have had many clients come to me being distrusting and only comfortable with a rare few people. When this occurrence was explored further, it was found that these individuals weren't readily comforted by their parents and were often left to self-soothe to unrealistic extents. Their need for comfort wasn't addressed, leaving them to regulate their emotions on their own, even though they had not reached the mental or emotional maturity to do so. As a result of this self-regulation, they were usually led to take a much longer time to calm down when they experienced any form of distress.

The anxious element in their attachment results in many of these individuals hesitating to let go of the person who isn't there to comfort them. They cling to this person even when their experiences show that the person wouldn't easily or readily comfort them.

The clients that I have worked with, whom I identified as having anxious-insecure attachments, were usually entirely thrown off track by changes in their lives. Moving houses left them highly emotional and almost unable to function rationally in their new space. This behavior mimics childhood behavior, where a child experiences reluctance to engage with others or explore new surroundings.

Avoidant-Insecure Attachment

In many instances, when children are playing in a public space, they will be playing and enjoying themselves but will often return back to their parent as a point of safety, whether it is for a hug or just to make sure that their parent is still there as a form of security. However, children with avoidant-insecure attachments are often found to willingly and openly engage with strangers and don't feel the need to return to their parents for any reason. They would much rather take care of their needs themselves than depend on a caregiver who has proven to be inconsistent in their caregiving and in attending to the child's emotional needs.

Disorganized-Insecure Attachment

Disorganized-insecure attachment often proves to be an extremely complex type of attachment in that an individual will often lash out and retaliate against the person from whom they so desperately seek comfort. In children, this attachment style is seen as children going to their parents for comfort but lashing out by screaming or kicking when the parent does try to comfort them or entirely ignoring the parent when the parent is near to them. In couples who have formed a romantic attachment, I have seen this style manifest with one partner desperately seeking out the attention of the other partner but retaliating and arguing when they do receive the attention they were seeking. This behavior often leads to unhappiness in the relationship.

Having insight into each of these forms of attachment not only allows you to see what the traits and characteristics of each one are, but it also allows you to identify this behavior in yourself and others, making it easy to deal with the root cause of our relationship issues.

In the next chapter, we will take a deeper dive into anxious attachments, and we will look closer at the emotional implications this attachment style leads to, not only on the one who experiences them but also on those around them.

CHAPTER 2

UNDERSTANDING ANXIOUS ATTACHMENT

Anxiety is something we have all experienced to some extent, and it is quite an unpleasant feeling. Symptoms like having your heart rate increase, your stress levels spike, and your breathing falter are enough to make anyone feel miserable. This is further magnified by the fact that, in most cases, many people experience these sensations around the people who are supposed to be closest to them.

Sometimes, the source of our greatest dismay is the anxiety we feel as a result of those closest to us. We develop a high threshold for anxiety, which often means we reach our mental and emotional breaking point before realizing it. We experience severe emotional and mental burnout without even recognizing it.

EMILY JOHNSON

Let us delve deeper into understanding anxious attachment and where it comes from.

Anxious attachments usually form one of two extremes on the attachment scale. People who have anxious attachments either find themselves being excessively needy or entirely withdrawn. Consider this example: As a child, if your parent was distant all the time and was never available to meet your mental and emotional needs, you may find yourself either having a great fear of abandonment later in life, which causes you to cling to people, or your fear of abandonment forces you to rely on no one but yourself, leading you to isolate yourself.

Both of these extremes prove to be detrimental to us and our well-being. Let us first look at the scenario of an overly needy person. Neediness can present in different ways. There are obviously people who are needy because they cannot fulfill their own basic needs, such as a young child, but neediness in the context of this book is what stems from attachment issues.

When someone is excessively needy, particularly as an adult, they demand your time and attention, their happiness and satisfaction are usually dependent on how much you focus on them, and they need constant reassurance that you are committed to them and that you care for them. They can become entirely dependent on you not only to meet their physical needs but also to meet their mental and emotional needs, which can become frustrating and taxing on you.

However, it is important to realize that whenever this neediness is exhibited by someone close to us, it is not a fault of their own, but it is a result of an anxious attachment style. Neediness could be exhibited through a fear of being alone, for a short while or forever (in a romantic relationship, this neediness may lead to a person having a constant fear or insecurity that their partner is going to leave them), a need for constant closeness and affection, engaging in attention-seeking behaviors that include positive and negative attention, they have low a self-esteem and self-worth, and they are codependent making them reliant on others to a large extent. When they are placed into a position of being entirely self-sufficient, they often fail in exaggerated ways *(Madel, 2022)*.

For example, someone may be dependent on their romantic partner to take them to and from work despite their partner needing to get to their own job in a different location. The person who grew up with an anxious attachment may have their driver's license but, when forced to drive themselves, gets lost along the way, finding themselves in difficult and dangerous situations despite having the tools needed to get to their destination successfully.

People who are needy also tend to be more jealous and untrusting, even with the people they have been in relationships with for long periods of time. They are untrusting of the people around their partner, and they are even untrusting of their partners. This lack of trust is something that ultimately causes the demise and the inevitable downfall of their relationships, despite them being aware that trust is the foundation of every long-lasting relationship.

Aside from the above-mentioned attributes, neediness is also seen in the following habits:

- They are often driven by their insecurities which usually leads to them making decisions that are not healthy for either them or their partner.
- They also find it extremely difficult to make decisions despite their decisions being made based on their insecurities. They always ask for advice, even if they don't follow the advice.
- They constantly need validation and often value the opinions of others above all.
- They fear isolation or being alone.
- They find it difficult to communicate what they are feeling and why. Overall, their communication fixates on their insecurities, and despite the constant need to talk to their partners, their contact lacks essence.
- They also show excessive tendencies of over-reacting and manipulating their partner, often by trying to pin the blame on their partner.

On the other end of the spectrum exists extremely withdrawn behavior. This behavior comes from the parent-child relationship and inconsistency from the parent which leads to the child feeling overly self-reliant. This forced independence is not beneficial because the child becomes excessively withdrawn, and they often don't ask for help or share their difficulties, even when the burden is too heavy for their shoulders.

As a young child, when they develop an unhealthy level of independence, they may experience several negative effects as a result of not having someone to depend on or talk to, even if it is of their own volition. They may experience anxiety, symptoms of depression, and internalizing their stresses and difficulties. They may face bullying and victimization because of their withdrawn and anti-social behavior, and they may face difficulties in a school setting whereby they find it difficult to engage with teachers.

As these individuals become adults, social isolation becomes harder to maintain. The effects of this isolation are entirely detrimental not only to their well-being but to their relationships as well. They avoid social events, they turn down invites, they purposefully try to be alone, and they make no effort to meet new people.

Someone who is withdrawn may also be social, but essentially, it is superficial, and they have a great fear that those around them will let them down. While they may have many friends, they make sure never to ask their friends for anything because of a disappointing relationship they would have had with their caregiver or parent as a child.

Anxious attachments, in most cases, cause people to have unhealthy relationships where they exhibit unhealthy patterns or stick to abusive relationships for fear of rejection. Considering that humans innately desire closeness and bonds with other people, we see that anxious attachment styles stand in the way of forming and developing the bonds we desperately need.

Origins of Anxious Attachment

Humans tend to enjoy labeling things in neat boxes or categories that define and identify the parameters of our lives. However, labeling is not easy to do in reality. When we look at someone's childhood and pause to consider the reasoning behind why they developed an anxious attachment style in their adulthood, we are inclined to think that one or all of the possible causes are what set them off on the path and trajectory on which they find themselves.

However, someone may experience only one trigger that causes them to develop this form of attachment style, while others may be subjected to a wide array of causes that lead to them forming anxious attachments later in life.

We are still left with the question of what exactly causes anxious attachments in adults and what must occur in one's childhood that leads to the development of anxious attachment as an adult. While this attachment style is usually exhibited in adult relationships, it is caused at a very young age.

Experiencing any of the below scenarios as a child can cause you to develop anxious attachments as an adult *(Brennan, 2021)*:

- **Trauma:** While it is often not immediately recognized, many people experience trauma to different extents. Trauma is the response or the lingering feeling that we experience when something negative happens to us. It can be caused by minor events such as a bad experience on the first day of school that leads to the child not wanting to go to school the next day to extreme cases of abuse, abandonment, violence, crime, or natural disasters. The way trauma affects each person is different. For some, they may suppress it while parts of it subtly seep into their attachments and relationships. For other people, it may become their entire identity, and they explicitly use it as the reason they experience challenges in their relationships.

- **Neglect:** When a child is neglected, they receive no care. Depending on the extent of the neglect, they may not experience emotional fulfillment, they may not experience mental and cognitive stimulation, and in extreme cases, they may not even know where their next meal will come from. The uncertainty of not knowing is where the anxiety in these children stems from.

- **Separation from parents:** We have already established the importance of the bond and attachment that exists between parents and children. If this bond is disrupted in any way, a child can go on to experience anxious attachments as an adult. Any form of separation from a parent at a young age can cause a child to experience fear. This fear can grow, leading to the child becoming overly cautious and fearful if their parent or anyone else leaves them. Separations that are caused by long hospital stays (with the child or parent being in the hospital), parents working far from the child, or the parent abandoning the child permanently can cause differing levels of fear and trauma in the child. This fear and trauma can even make short-term separations, such as going to work or weekends spent apart, extremely difficult.

- **Inconsistency from parents:** In every facet of life, children require consistency and routine. It's how they thrive. In terms of parental emotions, children require consistency too. This consistency means that even when parents have difficult days or are feeling emotionally worn out, they need to respond in a consistent manner to their children as they would on a good day. Parents need to be consistent because children learn to understand their parents' behaviors, they learn boundaries from what is established early on, and they feel safe in the consistent emotional responses they experience from their parents.

- **Depression in caregivers:** In most cases, the cause of anxious attachments in an individual stems from a problem in their childhood that wasn't controllable. This means that in situations of trauma or even a parent or caregiver experiencing depression, the child may grow up with certain insecurities. Depression stems from something that isn't easily controlled by the caregiver. Unintentionally, they cause anxiety in their child, which ultimately goes on to affect every future relationship the child experiences.

- **Inexperienced mother:** One of the more complex and unintentional causes of anxious attachment is a mother who is inexperienced. Now, the reality is that every woman is inexperienced before she becomes a mother, but this inexperience does not mean that every child, or first-born child, develops anxious attachments. Instead, when a mother chooses to ignore her instincts or chooses to succumb to the pressures of society when it comes to taking care of her baby, it may lead to anxious attachments. Something as simple as not responding to their baby's needs when they cry because they were told that they would be spoiling their child *(Cafasso, 2019)* or hindering their development can lead to anxious attachments forming later in their child's life.

These varying causes can affect an individual's development well into adulthood and can make them feel like they are trapped, even by experiences that they aren't entirely aware of. However, despite these causes that exist, we also need to consider individual and genetic differences that people have.

Consider a family with two parents and three children. The way each child is raised, their personality, the relationships they have with their parents and siblings, and their temperament is entirely different and unique.

I have often seen individuals who have anxious attachments, but they come from families where their siblings don't have the same experiences they do. Their fears and anxieties are their own. When we delve further into this concept, we find that even scientific research supports these major differences in family members.

At any point in life, we all change; the difference in our current environment is slightly developed or altered from a previous version of ourselves. These subtle and almost unnoticeable changes seep into the different facets of our lives and will ultimately impact how we interact with each person around us.

When a couple welcomes their first child, their relationship changes with each other changes. When they have another child, their relationships with each other, with their first child, and with their newborn will also change.

A study that assessed the attachment of siblings to their mother, *(van IJzendoorn et al., 2000)* found that there are differences in how each sibling is bonded with their parent. The study found that according to attachment theory, the attachment styles between siblings, whether they are boys or girls, are expected to be the same, provided parents remain consistent. However, because parents change their interactions with their children over a four-year period, a second child is more likely to display a different level of attachment security than the first-born child.

Another influencing factor that this study found to influence connections between children and their mothers is gender. Boys and girls tend to develop different attachment styles with their mothers to certain extents.

Family dynamics play an important role in how attachments develop, especially since this environment is the foundation for attachments to form. In addition to the dynamics that exist directly between the parent and the child, there is also the dynamic that exists between other family members that the child may be exposed to. These relationships can be both positive and negative.

Although secure attachment is the style to which most families, if not all, aspire, we need to understand the mechanisms that are at play and that can cause a disruption in the homeostasis of the family dynamic. Parents often think that their children are oblivious to the aspects that help keep a home in balance, but even subtle changes in the parents' stress levels can affect them.

Factors that can influence the family dynamic include the following examples *(MedCircle, 2021)*:

- The relationship between parents influences the overall family dynamic. If children observe a hostile, abusive, stressful, or strained relationship between the parents, they are likely to experience some form of anxiety as well.
- People outside of the nuclear family make decisions and control what occurs in a home, thus influencing what happens in that home.
- The relationships between siblings and between a person's parents and siblings will influence the overall dynamic.
- External factors such as finances, sociopolitical climates, and poverty play a part.
- A change or shift in the home dynamic, including divorce or separation, a new baby being born, or moving houses, will inevitably cause a shift in the dynamic.
- Major differences in the family, such as different cultures, races, and religions, influence the overall family dynamic.

Now that we have looked at the external influences that have the potential to cause anxious attachments in individuals, let us look at the intricate emotional web that is formed and the emotional complexities that it can cause.

Unraveling the Emotional Web

The emotional complexities caused by anxious attachment aren't always rational or easily explained. Imagine a spiral that goes infinitely downward. Having anxious attachments causes the very thing an individual fears to become their reality.

For instance, many people with anxious attachments in their relationships might experience these forms of attachment because of a fear of abandonment. Their father may have left the home when they were young or their mother may not have consistently met their emotional needs, which may have left them feeling emotionally unfulfilled. These occurrences create the fear of abandonment, which may cause them to become excessively needy and insecure when they find themselves in a romantic relationship. Depending on the person with whom they are in a relationship, they may push the other person away with their lack of trust and severe insecurity. This behavior leads them to feel more abandoned, and so the cycle continues.

However, these emotional complexities don't just exist in one's everyday relationship, with one partner constantly asking the other if they love them. Instead, it goes a lot deeper than that scenario and can be triggered by certain events or occurrences in a relationship.

Every relationship moves from one stage to the next, but a slight change, disruption, or even growth in the relationship can trigger someone's anxious attachments. Their anxiety grows when a new relationship begins when their relationship faces a milestone such as an anniversary, when there is general conflict in the relationship that naturally arises and could otherwise be easily resolved, and even when general stresses in life occur. Their anxiety spikes because they are ill-equipped to handle conflict, and they haven't experienced an environment that was safe or that portrayed healthy conflict resolution.

Because of their fear of abandonment, conflict has higher stakes and a greater value to someone who has an anxious attachment style. They find it hard to see the line between healthy conflict, which helps the people in a relationship communicate and understand their differences, and conflict that might lead to the relationship ending. In many cases, because of their severe anxiety, they will try to avoid or end conflict as soon as possible, even if the outcome is not desired or ideal.

But the complexities don't end with the person with anxious attachments and their partner. Every relationship is built on the foundation of trust, honesty, respect, and communication, and it is these pillars that make a relationship healthy and successful; however, anxious attachment styles attack each of these pillars, creating discord in the relationship. This behavior leads to anxiety seeping into the other facets of a relationship, and it inevitably leads to children (if there are any) experiencing this discord, creating the potential for another generation to be affected by anxious attachment styles.

Fear of Abandonment

To some extent, we all feel a fear of being left alone. We can face this fear of being alone for the rest of our lives or even for just a day or two when our home is empty. This feeling is real and can take control of every moment in our lives. This fear of being left alone is heightened in people with anxious attachment styles, so much so that they become fixated on not being alone and not being abandoned.

People who face anxious attachments may not even realize their fear of abandonment until they are in a romantic relationship. But what does this fear look like, and how can you identify this fear in yourself or others?

- People who have a fear of abandonment will often get into relationships extremely quickly. It will be almost as if they don't know someone, but they are already publicly dating. Friends and people close to them will caution them about getting into relationships too quickly, but they will often throw caution to the wind and give themselves entirely to a relationship that hasn't grown in value.

- Despite getting into relationships that appear too serious too quickly, they find it difficult to commit entirely. They often approach their relationships with a guarded heart, thinking that they would rather not get hurt by one person while not having any thought if they hurt someone with their lack of commitment. This behavior usually leads to them having a string of failed relationships that have never passed the three- or six-month mark.

- Because of their intense and deep-seated fear of being alone, they often don't spend much time between relationships which causes them to move on too quickly without addressing or dealing with any of the trauma they faced in their past relationships. They carry this hurt and trauma into their future relationships, which usually causes issues and leads to the ultimate end of those relationships too.

- Many people who face a fear of abandonment feel like they are unworthy of love and affection. Because they feel unworthy, their perception is that their partner also thinks they are unworthy. This feeling oftentimes leads to them getting jealous easily, engaging in unwanted sex to keep someone's attention, staying in difficult or abusive relationships, overthinking almost all situations, and repressing emotions as a way of avoiding conflict *(Fritscher, 2022)*.

People who have a fear of abandonment fight a constant battle in their head, and they seem to always be trying to find the perfect middle ground to be the perfect partner, even though their mind often gets the better of them. The very thing they fear causes them to experience abandonment over and over again, adding deeper layers to the trauma that has already formed in their childhood.

Most people have the innate ability to cope and adapt to the inevitable changes that life throws at us. But those with abandonment issues get trapped in their fear and find it nearly impossible to move on. If they face the loss of a loved one, they get trapped in that grief as they battle to come to terms with being abandoned by their loved one.

The complexities of anxious attachments and the fears that they cause are endless. This, coupled with the intricacies and the ever-changing landscapes that human life is subjected to, can make overcoming these difficulties seem impossible. However, overcoming these attachment styles is always within reach.

Now that we have an understanding of anxious attachment styles and the fear they pose in many people's lives, in the next chapter, we are going to delve into how this style affects a person's everyday life.

CHAPTER 3

THE IMPACT OF ANXIOUS ATTACHMENT ON EVERYDAY LIFE

As we endeavor to better understand anxious attachments, we often find that most of the available information is categorized by terms that serve as a diagnosis. As research and science expand on this topic, I have found a lot of information, especially in my career, to point to somewhat of a check-box type definition. But as you, dear reader, endeavor to identify these traits in your own life and in your own relationships, I have sought to present you with case studies that serve to help you better identify anxious attachments and how they present in everyday life.

There is a firm line that distinguishes between traits and characteristics that people may possess which cause them to have anxious attachments, and the traits and behaviors they portray in day-to-day life that may lead their loved one to suspect that they may have an anxious attachment style. In the below case studies, we will look at the emotional highs and lows that many people may experience when they have anxious attachments and what they may experience in different life situations. The theoretical framework is often different from real-life experiences.

As a benchmark and a point of reference as we look at the following case studies, let us consider what a normal attachment looks like and how it is formed. Consider a young female child at the age of about two or three years old. While sleeping one night, she has a nightmare and wakes up crying in her sleep. She calls for her mother, who is in the next room, and without skipping a beat, her mother is at her side within seconds, soothing her fear. As time goes on, this young girl develops a secure attachment to her parents, knowing that even though her parents head to work each day, they will return at a specific time.

As she grows older, she gets into her first serious romantic relationship. However, after two years of dating, she found out that her partner had been unfaithful. She is devastated and distraught. She mourns the loss of the man she loved and the relationships she held dear to her, but ultimately, she takes the time to work through the pain before getting into another romantic relationship. She faces a few more break-ups before finding the man she will marry. She is well-adapted and emotionally regulated, and while her life is not without struggles (she faces conflict with her husband, stress at work, the anxiety of raising her children, the loss of her dad, and taking care of her widowed mother), she manages to adapt and doesn't allow her anxiety to rule her.

This prime example shows us someone who has grown up in an environment of secure attachments; her emotional needs were always met, and she learned how to process her emotions.

If we look at the day-to-day emotions of a child with anxious attachments, as seen in previous chapters, their school lives may involve beginning each day by crying because of a fear of being separated from their parent. They may continue crying despite it being late in the school year. In the school setting, they find it extremely difficult to share with other children, and they usually end up in tears when forced to part ways with toys or other tools that are needed for a specific activity.

Once their day has ended and their parent arrives, they are again met with uncontrollable tears, and their parent is unable to calm them down. This situation poses feelings of ambivalence in that the child simultaneously cries for the parent while not being comforted by the presence of the parent.

Now that we have an understanding of the day-to-day activities and emotions that a child may experience or portray that lead them to develop an anxious attachment style, let us look at case studies from clients with whom I have worked.

Kaitlin is a 29-year-old female who is married with one child. During her childhood, Kaitlin faced intense abandonment. Her dad left her and her mom when she was only five years old, and her mother slipped into intense depression, leaving Kaitlin to fend for herself on a near-constant basis. She was forced to provide for herself, begging for food from neighbors.

As she got older, Kaitlin found herself in many unpleasant relationships, including ones that were filled with abuse and violence. However, her intense fear of being alone caused her to hang onto those relationships despite the toxicity. Eventually, she found the man that she would marry, but their relationship proved to be tumultuous.

During the month prior to their marriage, their relationship progressed as expected, with them growing together and their bond developing. However, after their marriage and within the first three months of moving in, Brian, Kaitlin's husband, noticed a few changes in her demeanor. Kaitlin had grown extremely insecure and constantly sought reassurance of his love for her. She desperately sought out affection, even in moments that weren't always appropriate (such as calling when he was in meetings). When Brian was unable to meet her emotional neediness or when he was unable to respond immediately to her calls and texts, he would come home to excessive hostility and intense arguments that usually ended with Kaitlin accusing him of infidelity.

Any changes in their lives would send her into an emotional flat spin that would either cause her to lash out aggressively, screaming and yelling in the home, or would lead to her experiencing depressive episodes where she would isolate herself alone in the bedroom, sleeping for the majority of the day.

Through these intense emotional highs and lows, of which Brian was the target for the most part, her daughter was present and watching her mom go through these extreme episodes. While Brian tried to make sure that their daughter was always taken care of and that her mental, physical, and emotional needs were all well met, she still witnessed the emotional highs and lows that her mother portrayed, and she felt the inconsistencies in the emotional support that her mother expressed toward her.

While Kaitlin could function quite well in a social environment and even in her career and professional life, her greatest problems were often presented when it came to Brian. At a social or family occasion, she would often be quiet and isolate herself, only to become upset when Brain was engaged in social pleasantries. If Brain wasn't constantly showering her with affection and attention or talking about her when in the presence of company, Kaitlin would quickly become insecure.

If Kaitlin and Brian had a disagreement in front of other people, it would cause an argument to brew that would even last days after the initial incident had occurred. During our counseling sessions, Brain often voiced his concerns about the extreme highs and lows in their relationship. He expressed that he often felt like he was not good enough. Working in a really demanding job that required him to be in contact with a wide array of clients left their relationship open to the emotional onslaught from Kaitlin, who was insecure about him being in contact with people she did not know, especially with female clients. Despite Brain's commitment and faithfulness to their relationship, Kaitlin would often accuse him of cheating or being disloyal, and this behavior, in turn, would lead to aggressive outbursts from Kaitlin.

In the absence of Brain, Kaitlin would often come across as extremely outgoing, talkative, and open to giving her details out to people she had just met. This change in demeanor led me to believe that two factors were coming into play here: either she was insecure about Brian getting more attention, or in his absence, she sought attention from others.

Looking at Kaitlin's behavior, responses, and emotional reactions, it was clear to see that she, Brian, and their child were not experiencing the emotional satisfaction that would have come from a secure attachment style. While the underlying cause for her behavior did stem from a fear of abandonment, something she had experienced from her father at a young age, she also had extremely low self-esteem and self-worth.

Self-Esteem and Self-Worth

How does the fear of abandonment relate to low self-esteem and self-worth? Well, when we look at the example above, the three facets are interrelated because Kaitlin's fear of abandonment was firmly set in place at a very young age. But as the human mind is inclined to think more about the negative than the positive, Kaitlin's mind is forced to wonder if it was her fault or something that she did to cause her father to leave.

Kaitlin began blaming herself or often spent time wondering if her situation was her own fault. Constantly wondering if it was her own actions or behavior that made her father leave led her to develop biases against herself. She thought that it must be something she did that caused her father to leave, and if it was, she needed to be sure not to make that mistake again, lest she face the emotional loss of someone abandoning her again.

In trying to take control and prevent herself and her daughter from experiencing the emotional turmoil that comes from a parent leaving or abandoning you, Kaitlin overcorrected. She would try to show Brian how overly dependent she was on him while also trying to ensure she could survive entirely without him. Being pulled in these two opposing directions caused her to experience intense extremes of both emotions. She also caused her own mental harm by conjuring up false impressions and images about Brian despite knowing confidently that he was a good man who always treated her well and respected her.

How does her behavior reflect this duality? Well, in the case study above, we have seen Kaitlin exhibit this behavior in one of two ways: first, she will lash out and act out in ways that push Brian away as a way of guarding her own feelings and emotions, and second, she would become excessively involved in his interactions to consistently remind him of her presence.

Because she had low self-esteem, she would feel insecure about not being good enough for Brian, but would also try to prove to herself that she was good enough by seeking attention from others, especially in Brian's absence.

Anxious attachment leaves most people with a poor perception of themselves which leads to low self-esteem and low self-worth. Our self-esteem, while it is something that we feel about ourselves, is influenced by a lot of external factors. Yes, it is categorized by how we value ourselves, how we feel about ourselves, and the confidence we have, but as we interact with other people on a daily basis, they will ultimately influence how we perceive ourselves. For the most part, our self-esteem is highly based on our self-awareness and our ability to recognize our abilities and inabilities. Our self-esteem is based on the type of person we are, our beliefs, our abilities, our weaknesses, our goals, and the people with whom we surround ourselves.

When we value someone, and we value their thoughts and opinions, they have greater power in influencing our self-esteem. This power is why the role of the caregiver and parent is so profound in which attachment types people develop. When someone you value abandons you or tells you something negative about yourself, you may find yourself fixated on that one aspect. This process ultimately affects our self-esteem.

However, one thing that can be noted is that one's self-esteem consistently moves back and forth on a continuum. Some days we may feel more confident and positive, while other days we may find ourselves in a slump. But it is this self-esteem that may affect our emotions and behaviors at different moments, as we can see in the above scenario with Kaitlin.

Our self-worth is what determines whether or not we see ourselves worthy of being loved. This feeling comes solely from within.

Our self-worth is determined by our self-evaluated abilities. It's us drawing a conclusion about ourselves based on our evaluation of how we complete tasks and our performance on tasks that we hold in high regard. If we value money and we are really good at budgeting or managing our finances, our self-worth will go up. But what is important to note is that there are different ways that we all measure our self-worth.

In Kaitlin's instance, her self-worth was often measured by the attention she received, whether it was from Brian, whom she valued, or from others in a social setting, whose opinion she also valued.

Identifying Anxious Attachments

It is easier to look at others with an objective point of view and identify the behaviors that would qualify as anxious attachment styles, but when it comes to ourselves, because we live in our own minds, this behavior can be quite hard to identify. For example, recognizing if we are needy or anxious isn't easy, especially when this seems to be our default mode or we feel the same way consistently on a daily basis.

If you find yourself experiencing thoughts of extreme desperation or neediness, thoughts that may seem irrational to others but seem perfectly normal to you, you may find that you have an anxious attachment style.

To some extent, we all face insecurities. However, when our insecurities control our lives, when they become the source of the conflict and turmoil in our relationships, and when every argument comes back to our anxiety and our insecurities, it is a sign that the attachments we have with our partners are formed based on our anxieties.

I have often had clients tell me that they try to rationalize the irrational thoughts in their minds. They will face a near-constant internal conflict where they recognize their behavior as irrational, but they constantly seek to validate the irrationality, defending their feelings about why they may be entitled to be needy, dependent, or insecure. This mindset often feels like blaming their loved one for the mistakes of others, which proves to be extremely detrimental to relationships in itself.

Most people keep two important facets of their lives separate: their past and the behaviors and actions of the present. They attempt to keep these two parts of themselves different, isolating the one from the other in an attempt to eliminate cause and effect. Because they try to rationalize their behaviors and their insecurities, and because they often brush away or suppress the inconsistencies they experienced as a child, they don't easily see the link between the two. It is only when they are inclined to seek help and when they are forced to confront their past after those around them have seen their hurt that they are forced to come face-to-face with their anxious attachment.

Trying to rationalize your insecurities or finding that the source of conflict in your relationship is a result of your own behavior may be the first signs that you have an anxious attachment style. The next step from here would be to allow yourself some introspection and retrospection for you to consider your childhood and your past. While it is a scary thing to consider doing and something that may terrify you, coming face-to-face with the very thing that caused us to face anxiety in our relationships is also the thing that is going to help us identify and remedy the issues we face in our relationships.

Identifying our own faults or shortcomings is not easy to do. However, it usually is the first step toward recovery and toward making better choices about our relationships. This inner work, in turn, will ultimately heal the scars we have and that have formed in our relationship.

Understanding the Fear of Abandonment

If you are identifying anxious attachments in yourself or in someone close to you, the most important thing to realize is that your feelings, fears, and anxieties are real—they stem from a real place and are valid. Now, it is about working through those feelings.

The fear of abandonment is often categorized by the notion of being once bitten and twice shy. It is a fear that stems from deep within that has been etched in our minds because we have once been abandoned, and we are going to do everything in our power to stop it from happening another time.

A fear of abandonment can affect the decisions you make in everyday life. It can cause you to overcompensate in your relationships by overcorrecting in either direction. Sometimes, if you have a fear of abandonment, you may exhibit a variety of behaviors and emotions, as seen below *(Darcy, 2016)*:

1. You find it near impossible or extremely difficult to experience any form of intimacy with someone. You may find it hard to allow someone into your life entirely, or perhaps you even try concealing parts of yourself away from others. The reason for this behavior is that most people would rather not be rejected for who they are authentically. Pretending to be someone else or concealing parts of yourself allows the world to see only what you choose, and if they reject you on that basis, well, then it wasn't the real you to begin with.

2. You create an inauthentic version of yourself. This version in itself is something that gets deeply distorted on an internal level. After years and years of weaving a false image of who you are (because you never truly allow people to get to know you and love you), you may begin questioning if people actually love you at all.

3. Your innate and core beliefs, and the beliefs that make you intrinsically you, are all based around your abandonment. This means that a core belief that you have is that you can't trust others. You may believe that everyone is only temporarily in your life, or you may believe that you are not someone who is easily loved by others.

4. You feel lonely in a relationship, even though you are with someone you have fallen in love with. This is because you often find that you choose not to give your

ANXIOUS ATTACHMENT RECOVERY

all to a person for fear that they may abandon you at some point in the future. You try to protect parts of you, but because you can't be entirely you, you find yourself alone with the parts of you that you try to hide.

5. And finally, you may find yourself stuck in repetitive motions. You find yourself ending up in relationships that all head down the same path, with you being abandoned in the very same way that initially caused your first trauma. This repetition leads to your wounds getting deeper and deeper. But why does this happen? Well, we revisit the same things that caused us the initial hurt because we are drawn to aspects of familiarity. We end up predisposed to choose the devil we know rather than the devil we don't.

The fear of abandonment has the power to shape, mold, and morph not just our romantic relationships but our familial bonds and the relationships we form in every other aspect of our lives.

I get it; sometimes, protecting ourselves is more important than allowing us to feel something that only has the potential to be great. But when you learn that abandonment is a roadblock that prevents you from feeling the love you deserve, you allow yourself the opportunity to overcome the very thing that causes you to blame people in your life for the mistakes of others.

In general, it is not easy for us to see or identify how anxious attachments and abandonment can influence our daily lives. But here is where the element of introspection, coupled with communication with those around us who see the detrimental effects of our behaviors on our connections, comes into play. It can lead to the healing that comes with seeking health.

Without recognizing what this anxious attachment style does to us, we will spend the rest of our lives in relationships that don't bring forth any form of happiness or fulfillment. We also risk creating a cycle where those around us, such as our children, develop the potential to form similar attachment styles. Once these changes and recognition come to the forefront of our minds, we are able to work through remedying the issues that plague our relationships.

In the next chapter, we are going to look specifically at romantic relationships and how anxious attachments can affect them. We will look at how romantic relationships are formed, what a secure attachment style in a romantic relationship looks like, and how an anxious attachment compares.

CHAPTER 4

ANXIOUS ATTACHMENTS IN ROMANTIC RELATIONSHIPS

Love is an absolutely beautiful thing, and when experienced in the appropriate context, it can be quite fulfilling—it can feel like you have found a part of yourself that was empty. Experiencing love in a romantic relationship can truly make you feel like you can take on anything in the world, but the reality is that we often mimic what we already know in our relationships.

It is a well-established notion that, as a parent, you set the tone for how your child will develop romantic attachments. For that reason, as a couple, parents are often encouraged to treat each other well with love and affection, especially in front of their children. They are encouraged to teach their children what a healthy relationship should look like, and ultimately, it is up to them to teach their kids what to expect and what to give to a partner. Parents are also encouraged to resolve conflict in front of their children because, to some extent, it allows their child to observe and develop conflict resolution skills that are needed for a romantic relationship to thrive.

When we see that parents help individuals establish healthy romantic relationships, we can safely assume that the same goes for unhealthy relationships and toxic bonds that are formed.

Patterns of Love

We all aspire to have healthy romantic relationships in our lives, not just because it brings us happiness and satisfaction but because it is the most important relationship we will have in our adult years. It also will be the example that generations to come will follow as their ideal relationship.

However, how do you know if you are in a healthy relationship? After all, people always say that every relationship has their issues. So how do you differentiate and decide if you are in a healthy relationship that faces expected challenges or if your challenges are all-consuming? Well, to know if your relationship is not working, you first need to know what a healthy relationship looks like.

A healthy relationship is one that exhibits the following five signs *(Eugene Therapy, 2022)*:

1. **Trust:** Trust is the foundation of every healthy relationship. Realistically, you aren't going to be with your partner every second of every day. Trust does go beyond the scope of insecurity. It isn't just about being comfortable with your partner being away from you, but it is also about knowing that there is a bond between you and your partner that allows you to share your secrets, concerns, and emotions safely with someone who truly cares for you. Our trust stems from the attachment styles that we form with our parents. Our trust will easily be waivered by our anxiety and by the example that our parents have set for us. Trust is also established over a long period of time, so as a healthy relationship grows, the trust you have with your partner will grow as well. Trust is built on the foundation of sharing, being open and honest, and allowing your partner into your mind and heart.

2. **Respect:** When you realize that a relationship comprises two equal humans joining together in unity, you realize what respect truly is. It is about seeing each other as equals, being kind to each other, and being involved in the things that make people happy. Respect is something that is present from the moment a relationship begins. We have an innate respect for our fellow humans, and this respect grows into different forms as your partner fulfills different roles in your life.

3. **Honesty:** Going hand-in-hand with trust, honesty forms a part of a healthy relationship in that you are openly and comfortably sharing aspects of your life with your partner. In reality, this means that you do have your own personal space, but if there is anyone you'd like to share your thoughts and feelings with, it would be with your partner.

4. **Affection:** While love and affection are present in all of our relationships to some extent, there is a type of intimate affection in a romantic relationship that is set apart from any other relationship you will have. While this is not the act of making love or sexual intimacy, there is a way in which you share yourself with your partner that is different from any other person in your life. When this pillar of your relationship falls apart, chances are the health of your relationship may be declining.

5. **Communication:** Unfortunately, without communication, none of the other pillars within your relationship can be established. This means that communication is the way you build trust, the way you initiate affection, the way you can be honest with each other, and how you show respect. Communication allows you to grow together and to see how you develop and change into each new version of yourself that exists. This is one of the joys that exist when you grow together and openly communicate as a couple.

A healthy relationship is made of two people aspiring to be the best versions of themselves for the person they love. In a healthy relationship where both people experience a secure attachment style growing up, they are both likely to have a healthy bond and relationship with each other.

However, people with an anxious attachment style experience romantic relationships in a different way. When they are in a romantic relationship, love for them is defined as being constantly fawned over, having someone's attention on them at all times, and constantly being told how much they are loved.

The ideal romantic relationship of someone who has anxious attachments is one where they receive the closeness and intimacy that they so desperately require from their partner. In their mind, their partner will constantly reassure them that they are the only one for them, that they are loved, and their partner will give them constant attention. They seek validation, so for their relationship to be considered perfect, their partner will need to tell them that they are perfect in every way. They need to know that their partner feels blessed to have them and that they are the best thing that has ever happened to them, even if it's not something rational for their partner to say constantly.

They also tend to value words more than actions. So while their partner constantly reassures them that they love them, their partner may not treat them well. But they stay with their partner because of the words and not because of their actions.

Despite having their partner constantly validate their feelings, they will still find themselves anxious and insecure about their relationship with their partner. If their partner has set a precedent of meeting their emotional needs and easing their insecurities, a situation may arise when, for some reason, their partner can't validate their feelings at a particular time. This situation could be something as simple as them being busy at work, but it has the potential to send their partner on a downward emotional spiral, sending their insecurities sky-high. However, being in a relationship with someone who has an anxious attachment style usually means that you will never have to question their feelings toward you. They are people who wear their emotions on their sleeves and are extremely emotionally expressive. In most cases, the partner of someone with an anxious attachment will know exactly what they are feeling at any given point *(Davis, n.d.)*.

This concept brings to mind the relationship of a couple who used to come to me for therapy—Bonnie and Damian. By all accounts, they had a pretty perfect relationship. To the naked eye, they were happy and utterly in love with each other, but it was behind closed doors that they faced their greatest challenges. However, it wasn't as easy to identify that they had an issue in their relationship, even to them. Damian often commented that their greatest rife was when he was occupied by his career. Given the nature of his job, Damian found himself extremely busy at least once a month. Every other time, they were in love, he would give her endless attention, and she would thrive off the consistent validation and affection that he gave her.

ANXIOUS ATTACHMENT RECOVERY

She commented that he was the one who never took hours to respond. He was always there...until he wasn't there. Working in the finance field, Damian found his work more demanding as each month came to a close when reports needed to be submitted, financials needed to be concluded, and salaries needed to be paid. This was the busiest time of his month, and he wouldn't have any time to respond to Bonnie. It was during these moments that her insecurities would rise and bubble to the surface. She would become insecure, questioning him and asking him if there was someone else, despite him doing everything in his power to reassure her that he was entirely committed to her. Bonnie would feel ignored and like she wasn't good enough, and in those moments, she would find herself wondering if she was doing the right thing and being the right partner for Damian.

For Damian, the first few instances that this situation had happened, he found himself genuinely concerned. But after it had persisted for the duration of their five-year relationship, it became troublesome for him. He felt like Bonnie didn't trust him and that, after five years, there was nothing he could do to earn her trust. However, he was often the one to tell me that being loved by Bonnie was one of the best things he had ever experienced. He often told me just how much he loved being loved by her. She was kind and affectionate and openly expressed her love for him. He often said that he never thought they had an issue in their relationship, but at every month's end, their relationship would face a hurdle. In our one-on-one sessions, Damian would often admit to feeling defeated in their relationship because of Bonnie's attachment style. He would express that he wished he hadn't set the bar so high in terms of constantly giving her affection, validation, and reassurance.

After weeks of therapy, individually and as a couple, they were able to overcome their issues, not because Damian reassured Bonnie once again of his loyalty, commitment, and feelings but because they dealt with the root of the problem, which was Bonnie's anxious attachment. Through therapy, they were able to uncover just how this anxious attachment style in Bonnie was formed, and she was able to work through and overcome the issues it posed in her romantic relationship with Damian.

The Struggles for Love

Everyone wants to experience deep and intense love. Of everything else that we experience in this world and in our lifetimes that is mediocre and mundane, love should not be one of them. But love is a strange notion, and it's not one that is easily and simply found. It takes finding an absolute stranger who is compatible with you and then starting a converged journey of life. No matter what intentions you have with a romantic partner, whether it is to get married, have children, or just spend your lives together on your own, you need to find someone with whom your life is going to intertwine.

How many times have you heard the phrase "baggage?" This term is often used socially by people to refer to anything that someone else might bring to a new relationship. The truth is, we all have baggage, whether it is from previous relationships, from our childhood, or from the temporary stress that we all seem to be facing in life. But a part of the complexity of finding love is the fact that we have baggage and that it affects us and the relationship we hope to have.

Specific to the context of this book, people with anxious attachments have their own unique baggage to deal with in a romantic relationship. Not only do they have to deal with their own emotions and the unique contrast of feelings that pull them in different directions, such as deeply yearning for a relationship but being terrified of being hurt or abandoned, but they also need to navigate the vulnerability that comes with allowing someone into your life and into your heart.

The scary thing about the challenges someone with anxious attachment faces in a romantic relationship is that they are often unaware of their attachment issues. Even before getting into a relationship, there are fears of abandonment, the inability to trust a partner entirely, and whether or not they are good enough for a partner *(Schuster, 2023)*.

Let us take a closer look at these challenges and begin to unpack them.

When someone has an anxious attachment style, they are faced with challenges in a relationship even before they get into a romantic relationship. It starts with the conflict of having a deep yearning to be in a relationship. You may even find someone with whom you would like to start a relationship or who you think is someone you are compatible with. But then, at the back of your mind, questions start creeping up. You wonder what type of person they are, and because you already have low self-esteem, you start wondering why they would be interested in you. You wonder if there is something wrong with you or with them because your perception of yourself is distorted and because you are untrusting of them. If they tell you that they had a failed past relationship, your mind immediately starts wondering why someone as wonderful as them has failed relationships.

However, in the early days of a relationship, you are caught between two conflicting situations where first, you really want to be in a relationship. Because you so desperately want to be in a relationship, you tend to fall in love quickly. But here is where the conflict comes into play. You fall in love quickly, but there is a fear that your partner will leave you at any moment, coupled with a deep distrust that this all seems too good to be true.

Even before a romantic relationship begins, someone with anxious attachments tends to need consistent reassurance, which on its own can pose stressful burdens on a relationship that may lead to the relationship not being successful. But the cycle continues if the relationship isn't successful, further cementing the insecurities that the person with an anxious attachment experiences. When relationships are unsuccessful, their insecurities grow because, quite frankly, the person they loved proved to them that their insecurities were, in fact, correct and valid.

Should a relationship make it past the beginning stages, the person with insecure attachments will face difficulties later in the relationship. They will face the near-constant fear that their partner may leave them even if their partner has proven to them that this will not happen. Eventually, their insecurity has the potential to become a catalyst in their relationship.

The conflict that exists within the individual between the need to be in a relationship and being almost entirely guarded and insecure about themselves makes the entire situation around their romantic relationship far more complex.

The Fear of Abandonment

As a counselor, there have been so many instances where I have heard someone say that they don't want to get into a relationship because there aren't any good people around or they think everyone will hurt them and no one can be trusted. Even before they have found someone or given someone the opportunity to prove that not everyone will hurt them, they have already set a precedent and an expectation for hurt and pain.

The fear of abandonment is one way that people bring to life the reality of having people who will abandon them and betray them. In many cases, people with anxious attachment styles get into relationships, and they fall in love very fast. When they fall in love, they commit themselves entirely to their partner. For lack of a better phrase, they place all their emotional eggs in one basket. They become entirely dependent on their partner to fulfill all their needs—mentally, physically, and emotionally—which leads to an exponentially worse and more excruciating heartbreak if their relationship doesn't work out. They feel like their world has come crashing down because the one person to whom they have given everything has ultimately let them down.

The fear of losing everything all at once leaves them feeling like they can't trust anyone, which can create a strong sense of abandonment. As this fear grows, they often find themselves overcorrecting and trying to protect themselves from the potential of being hurt. Because they are so afraid of being abandoned, they either choose to abandon the relationship before they can get hurt (which leads to sabotaging their own relationships), or they avoid relationships entirely, neither of which are beneficial.

How We Self-Sabotage Our Relationships

Our ruined relationships and the reason we sabotage our relationships are based on a number of driving factors, the first and most obvious of which is fear. We are afraid of being hurt, let down, and, most importantly, not being good enough. We also sabotage our relationships if we think we are not good enough, when we can't trust someone, or when we have expectations that are unrealistic or that ultimately set our partner up for failure. With these driving factors, we are more susceptible to ruining our relationships.

So how do we self-sabotage our relationships? There are a variety of techniques that people employ that ultimately prevent them from experiencing pain in their lives. These are considered destructive behaviors and are actively used to save themselves from the pain they are constantly afraid of *(Emamzadeh, 2021)*.

Some of the ways people sabotage their relationships are as follows:

- They pull themselves away from a relationship on a physical or emotional level. Physically, they pull away from their partner by limiting intimacy and spending more time apart than they do together. Emotionally, they display coldness and distance when they are together.
- They become defensive about simple aspects of the relationship. For example, if they spend time away from each other and their partner asks them about the distance they have been experiencing, they become defensive and retaliate by blowing the situation out of proportion. This can look like them asking their partner if they think they are cheating. They also turn constructive criticism or advice into something volatile, to which they respond with extreme victimization.
- They also attack their partner in some cases, which includes throwing accusations, insults, and blaming their partner for irrational things that happen in their relationship.

Further, we can see that a lot of people who sabotage their relationships do so from a place of fear. But this fear goes beyond the fear of abandonment. It goes deeper into the fear of engulfment and that, ultimately, they will lose themselves and their identity in a relationship. This comes back to the notion of putting everything you have into a relationship and feeling empty or like you have lost yourself in the relationship *(Fournier, 2023)*.

Additionally, when sabotaging their own relationships, people resort to extreme cases to force a relationship to end. From cheating, exhibiting extreme jealousy, and lying, their relationship comes to its inevitable demise.

However, at the basis of all these factors is the driving force of abandonment which stems from anxious attachment styles.

I have seen people who have been hurt and who have had their hearts broken beyond recognition, and yet still have a passion for love and finding a love that was meant for them. And then there are those who have been so brutally broken that they will never seek solace or joy from a relationship again. All of these testaments of love lost and found are meant to serve as a beacon of hope that even the most irreparable damage can be healed. But it comes with determination.

I have had clients who constantly seek love despite having been hurt in the past. There are those who have a fear of abandonment but are desperate to move past it. And then there are those who express their fears in entirely different ways.

I once had a client who explicitly told me that they sabotaged their own relationships because they didn't want to face a break-up or that they didn't want to be the one to end a relationship even when they had grown tired or bored of the relationship. This is yet another way in which anxious attachments contribute to the way a relationship is affected.

Because of the anxious attachment style that she was exposed to as a child, she was forced to attend to her own needs or to withdraw entirely from people she thought might hurt her. This, coupled with her own fear of commitment, caused her to execute extreme actions to get out of a relationship.

The complexities that one experiences when they sabotage their relationships don't bring about happiness or satisfaction. Instead, it brings about intense feelings of being ripped apart, destined to experience the heartache that they cause themselves.

But this is not the life that these individuals are sentenced to. In fact, they can go on to develop healthy, long-lasting relationships that aren't destined to be doomed or even sabotaged by themselves if they take the time to heal themselves.

So how do they stop themselves from sabotaging their relationships?

1. The first step is to recognize that you are sabotaging your relationship. Once you are aware of this fact, you can then work on changing the very thing that is causing your unhappiness.
2. Next, you need to take accountability. Once you do so, you admit to yourself that you are standing in your own way of a successful relationship.
3. You can then move on to identifying what it is about your relationships that trigger you into sabotaging them. It is here that you will work on identifying your fear of abandonment and realizing what exactly is the driving force behind your self-sabotage.

4. You need to be able to share your feelings in your relationship in a safe way. This means telling your partner that you recognize what it is that you're doing and that you need to work through it to save your relationship. It can also mean working with them through the difficulties you face and even seeking professional help if necessary *(Anwar, 2023)*.

At the end of every tunnel is a light. The light represents a brighter version of ourselves, it represents happiness and the ultimate joy that we have the potential and the right to feel. In the next chapter, we are going to make our way down the path of healing, looking closely at how you can overcome the anxious attachments that have been plaguing different parts of your life.

CHAPTER 5

OVERCOMING ANXIOUS ATTACHMENT

Healing is something that is equally as complex as the challenges we face in our anxious attachments. Healing is not a linear processor a final destination—and it is something that, when it is achieved, you don't immediately recognize it.

In the journey toward becoming a better version of yourself, you will find yourself facing the very things that have stood in the way of you experiencing relationships exactly the way you were meant to. You will find yourself on a journey toward healing, but one of the complexities of healing is that not everyone will accompany you on your journey. While you are facing world-altering changes, the world is still continuing as it always has. It is up to you to embrace the change that has been set in place for your advancement and block out the noise that seeks to drown you out.

EMILY JOHNSON

Let us look at why healing is so complex:

- At its very foundation, healing doesn't have a guidebook or clear instructions on how to go about achieving it. Add to this the fact that everyone has their own healing journey, it makes it even more complex because someone else's guidance or advice may prove to be futile to you.
- There also isn't a time frame in which you can achieve healing. It is far out of reach for some people and right around the corner for others. But neither timeline is wrong. Because it is a journey unique to each person, the timeline that you can expect your healing journey to take is immeasurable.
- Healing isn't a linear process. This means that you don't just move from one stage to the next until you come out fully healed on the other side. There are days when you might feel like you are failing, when you might feel like you have been unsuccessful in your healing endeavors, or when you might feel like you are doing worse than you were the day before. There are also days when you are going to feel like your anxiety is greater than it was even before you started pursuing your healing journey. Just because you aren't on your expected trajectory toward your healing goal doesn't mean that you are stuck or not healing at all.
- You might have heard this statement before, and I am going to say it again: healing is not a destination but a journey. It is something you constantly strive toward, something you work hard to achieve, and something

that you pursue relentlessly. After years and years of feeling like you are healed, you might come across a triggering situation that causes you to fight the battle against your trauma one more time. This doesn't mean your healing was unsuccessful, and it doesn't mean that you have failed or let yourself down; all it means is that you are still on your journey of healing.

- Many people are under the misconception that when you heal, it drops like a stone in your soul, immediately giving you peace and telling you that you were successful on your healing journey. This outcome is not entirely true. Healing is a combination of dealing with and getting over the emotional trauma you have faced that caused your anxious attachments. It is about making space for these past experiences to exist in your life while you learn to adapt and grow around your pain. You don't wake up one morning and realize that you're healed. Instead, you wake up one morning, remembering the pain, the trauma, and the triggers, but you realize that you aren't hurt or triggered anymore. You can smile at the pain of the past and move on in a healthy and happy way.

Addressing Anxious Attachments

This stage of understanding and working through your anxious attachment might be intimidating because it is here where you come face to face with the very thing that has been negatively affecting your relationships. It is time for you to go on the journey of addressing and confronting your anxious attachment style in a healthy way that ultimately leads to growth and not to pain and trauma.

Step 1: *Identify the anxious attachments you have been experiencing.*

This process is something I set as the benchmark for all my therapy sessions, and it is the benchmark I am going to set for you, dear reader, as you embark on the journey—in fact, you are already halfway there with step one because here you are, reading this book.

Identifying anxious attachments is not easy. But think about it this way, if you didn't notice a hole in your life, you would have never sought to fill it. Now that you have found and noticed the hole in your life, you can begin the journey to patch the hole up. You have identified that you or someone you love has an anxious attachment style, and now you can navigate your way through the healing process.

Once you recognize and face the anxious attachment style that you are confronted with, you can acknowledge that it exists, and you can work toward remedying it. You are no longer ignoring it and accepting your failed relationships as an unfortunate hand of fate.

Step 2: *Look to others to guide you as you regulate your emotions.*

This step is tricky to take because you don't want people manipulating your emotions. This means that you need to be careful in the way you approach others when you are trying to regulate your own emotions because it is you who controls your emotions and not anyone else. However, this step entails looking to others to best regulate the emotions and insecurities that seem to run away from you when you are highly anxious.

This step is particularly beneficial if you are already in a romantic relationship and you can communicate your feelings, emotions, and insecurities, and you can learn how your emotions and reactions may affect the partnership you have in your relationship. This advice does not mean that you should stop feeling emotions because it makes your partner uncomfortable, but it is rather about uncovering what makes them uncomfortable and how you can work on your emotional reactions. Perhaps what used to be an emotional outburst can now be a calm discussion because you have learned how to regulate your emotional responses from your partner.

Step 3: *Learn from a healthy example.*

Sometimes the best way for us to learn how to overcome our anxious attachment style is to learn from people who have grown up in an environment that harbored and nurtured a secure attachment style in their life.

You may find that you have friends who engage in relationships in an entirely different way than you do. You might also be in a relationship with a partner who has a secure attachment style. Use these relationships as an example from which you can learn.

This advice does not mean that your emotions, responses, and feelings need to mirror theirs. Instead, it means that you can better identify where you may be overreacting or responding in an unhealthy way to certain triggers. It is also important to discern the type of behaviors and emotional regulation that is healthy and beneficial for you. Just because someone always looks calm and seems to respond in just the perfect way doesn't mean that they are without their own trauma.

To know if someone truly has secure attachment styles and to know if they are someone you can look up to, you need to see their interactions between all their relationships. You can learn a lot from someone who has secure attachments, including the following examples:

a. How to set boundaries
b. Know when and how to say no
c. Realize that your emotions are valid and can be openly and safely shared
d. Understand that your past is your past, but your present and future can be changed and perceived differently

e. Know that emotional support and closeness are healthy and much-needed facets of every relationship

Step 4: *Deal with your past emotions instead of ignoring them.*

The reason why anyone has an anxious attachment style is because of a lack of attention or love received from their parents as a child. This inattentiveness from your parents is something that needs to be dealt with immediately and in a healthy way. Addressing the feelings of the past is one way of remedying the future interactions and relationships you will have.

You need to step back and ask yourself if your partner has done anything to evoke your insecurities or if you are blaming them for the hurt you have experienced in the past. When you confront your past, you allow yourself to identify if it is you who is having difficulties regulating your emotions or if it is your partner who has done something to evoke extreme emotional responses from you.

The reality is that even though we all aim to look forward and never live in the past, the past is what sets the tone for our future. Confronting our past makes sure that it doesn't have a hand in negatively dictating the way we live our lives in the future.

Step 5: *Equip yourself with the resources you need to overcome your anxious attachments.*

> When you equip yourself successfully, you not only develop the appropriate coping mechanisms to overcome your anxious attachments, but you also remind yourself that you are worthy of love and affection. This, in turn, helps you function well in the face of adversity that is often posed by life.
>
> Equipping yourself means understanding that you are worthy of love, affection, and kindness, and it helps you control your emotions, respond in appropriate ways, assist you in calming down, and helps you manage emotional outbursts and stressful situations.

Step 6: *Build up your self-esteem and realize what you are worthy of.*

> It is absolutely heartbreaking and entirely unfortunate that people with anxious attachment styles and insecure attachment styles experienced this way of life in childhood. It means that from a very young age, they were taught that they were not worthy, not good enough, and they weren't shown love and affection in the right way. As an adult, they now have to work through undoing and overcoming those feelings, and they need to learn that they are worthy, they are lovable, and they deserve more than what they have become accustomed to.

They need to learn that it is unhealthy to constantly expect their partner to leave or abandon them. They also need to realize that there is a great chance that they find someone who never wants to leave them, so always expecting that person to leave will cause more harm than good in their relationship.

As hard as it is, once you learn who you are and how much you are valued, you realize that you are worthy of the love you might have been afraid of.

Step 7: *Don't be ashamed to ask for help.*

Sometimes, we can't do this healing journey on our own, and sometimes, it isn't even for our partners to help us through the healing. Sometimes, our healing is a journey that we take by ourselves with the help of a professional. In these cases, seeking therapy or help from a professional is one of the best things you can do for yourself and to show yourself that you are worthy of love.

Seeking professional help and going to a therapist equips you with the coping mechanisms that you need to better regulate your emotions; it helps you face your past and your triggers in a safe space, and it allows you to see yourself through the eyes of someone else. This is often what we need for us to see that we are human and we are deserving of all the love in the world.

Addressing your anxious attachments is just one part of the healing journey. It is the first part of a longer journey. Once you have directly addressed and faced your anxious attachment, you have identified, sought help and guidance from others, and have realized your worthiness, you can then begin the next part of your journey, which is nurturing and fostering your own self-growth.

There are many ways for you to foster self-growth. Essentially, at its basis, self-growth is allowing yourself the opportunity to maneuver yourself free from the smaller space you once occupied and taking up the space that you deserve. No one is meant to stay small forever, and no one is meant to have their worth diminished. So how do you foster your own growth? Let us take a closer look below *(6 Ways to Develop a Growth Mindset..., 2019; Depierro, 2023)*:

- ***Establishing goals for yourself.***

  When you realize you deserve more and when you begin to grow and nurture your self-esteem, you realize that you are capable of achieving more in life and in your relationships.

  Unfortunately, this shift doesn't happen immediately or overnight. Instead, it takes effort on your part, and it is something you need to actively work toward. One way of achieving what you are worth is by setting and establishing goals for yourself. This practice helps you set criteria for your life and for what you deserve, which never allows you to accept anything less than what you deserve. When you set goals, you also have an ideal toward which you can work. This means that if you are overcoming the trauma of the past, you know that you are not going to get involved in relationships that continue the cycle of hurt and trauma.

You can set a goal for what you would like your next relationship to look like and work toward achieving that relationship. Your goals can also be personal and can be how you intend to build yourself up and treat yourself. Sometimes, before we can work on relationships with other people, we need to work on the relationships we have with ourselves. You could set goals that encourage you to be kinder to yourself, to show yourself more love, and to give yourself more affection.

- ***Embark on creating a growth mindset.***
  Working on adopting this mindset is a multifaceted approach to moving your mind forward as you overcome and overpower the confines that once held you in place. When you cultivate a growth mindset, you acknowledge that you have not reached your full potential, and the opportunity to do so lingers nearby. You tap into the vein of unexplored abilities, and you learn how to uncover your true potential.

It can look like trying something new that you have never done before, it can look like stretching yourself a bit further to see just how much more you can do, and it can look like giving yourself rest so that you can come back stronger and more powerful. Having a growth mindset means learning from your mistakes instead of dwelling on them. This leads to the next point...

- ***Learn from your mistakes.***

  It takes a lot of strength and willpower to admit that you have made a mistake, but how else are you able to learn from the mistake if you don't acknowledge that it has been done? Change your perception about what a mistake is. Instead of it being something disastrous, consider it an opportunity to learn. Take the time to backtrack on your experiences and see what you could have done differently and how you can approach the same problem once again.

  Failure only happens when you stop trying. If you never stop your attempts to succeed, you will continuously grow, and this continuous growth is what will help you as you move from strength to strength in your journey of healing.

- ***Embark on a journey of continuous learning.***

  Learning from your mistakes is just one part of a growth mindset. Once you learn from your mistakes, make sure you don't just stop there but that you embrace continuous learning. Make sure that you try to grow in different areas of your life. The truth is, we will never know everything in this world, and it is humbling to know and understand this. However, this means that we can be further motivated to grow who we are and what we know.

- *Pursue several paths of knowledge.*

  Yes, for the purpose of this book, I deeply encourage you to pursue emotional knowledge and to uncover a deep understanding of how you handle and process emotions. I encourage you to actively seek and pursue growth and development in the way you use and express your emotions. But growth comes from many additional aspects, all of which are beneficial to your emotional growth.

  For example, you could pursue deeper spiritual knowledge if that is something that you find interesting. Your spiritual well-being will directly be translated into your emotional well-being as well. You could pursue academic knowledge, the power of which will allow you growth and expansion in different areas of your life.

  Because our lives are so deeply and intricately linked, growth in one area impacts the growth we experience in other facets, which ultimately allows us to experience a greater potential in our lives.

- *Leave your comfort zones.*

  As strange as it might seem, the trauma that we have experienced in our childhood that led to us developing anxious attachment styles in our adulthood actually becomes a comfort zone in which we dwell. We don't grow because we wallow in our anxiety and insecurity. One way that we can come out of and remove those mindsets is by pursuing challenges, seeking changes, and actively finding ways of moving out of our comfort zones. These acts ensure that our experiences are vast, that we are able to respond appropriately to those experiences, and that we are equipped with the knowledge that we have acquired from those experiences.

- *Self-reflection.*
  Looking back on how far one has come is a way of ensuring that you always see how much you have grown. Self-reflection gives you the opportunity to take pride in your progress, reward yourself for how far you have come, and embrace the growth that you have experienced, no matter how uncomfortable it might have been.

Confronting your anxious attachments and making a concerted effort to move forward on a journey of continuous growth is just one aspect of your healing journey. Up until this point, you have faced the intangible parts of overcoming your anxious attachments. Now it is time to confront your demons and battle the things that hold you back head-on.

Healing Past Wounds

How do you resolve your childhood trauma and the issues you experienced as a child that ultimately affect you now as an adult? Doing this work is extremely difficult, especially because you don't have the younger version of yourself around to help through the healing journey. Instead, you are left with coping mechanisms that might not always be beneficial to your life as an adult.

While it is hard, the benefits of healing your past wounds are insurmountable. You get to heal the cause of your trauma while also venturing forth into your life with a new mindset. But how do you do it? How do you help heal a version of yourself that doesn't exist anymore but that has ultimately affected who you are now?

One of the most common ways of healing your childhood trauma is through therapy. Therapists provide you with a safe space that allows you to face your trauma without drowning under the triggers it may pose to you. They guide you through your healing process, ensuring that you are dealing with the wounds of the past without getting stuck in the past.

If you consider using therapy as a way of healing your childhood wounds, you may find that your therapist engages in talk therapy. Talk therapy is a way of safely sharing and talking about what you have faced as a child, pinpointing where exactly your trauma occurred, and safely confronting that trauma.

In addition to talk therapy, your therapist will equip you with tools and coping mechanisms that can be used when you feel like you are slipping down into a hole that is controlled by your past. Sometimes we get so fixated on the negative aspects of our past that we forget to look forward. This fixation leaves us trapped in our trauma and inevitably bound to repeat the cycle with those around us because we can't see beyond the hurt. However, having tools that help you cope gives you the opportunity to see beyond your hurt and is vital in making sure that you don't blame someone new in your life for the experiences that occurred in the past.

Additionally, a therapist will help you identify, confront, deal with, and let go of the trauma you experienced as a child. While it is impossible to undo the past, you can change your view and perception of your past. You can move from being a victim to being a victor. One of the greatest motivating factors I have seen in my clients that encouraged them to overcome their childhood traumas was that they didn't want to continue the cycle. They wanted to ensure that their kids never experienced the same trauma they went through, and the only way they could do so was by ensuring that they had dealt with the trauma themselves.

Sometimes, facing your childhood trauma can look like talking or journaling to your younger self. It can look like helping the child version of yourself get through the pain and heartache for the adult version of yourself to move forward in a happier way. While this may seem strange or weird, you need to realize that perhaps you were the adult you needed when you were growing up. One way of ensuring that you break the trauma cycle in your family is by making sure that you help yourself through the trauma. Be the person to yourself that you always needed.

Finally, dealing with your childhood trauma and healing your past wounds can look a lot like confronting your parents and bringing to their attention the hurt they may have unintentionally caused you. If this is part of the healing journey you choose to pursue, remember that your healing is your own. Remember that you cannot expect your parents to change, you should not expect an apology, and you should not expect them to acknowledge that they have caused you any hurt. Your healing is all about you. Speaking to your parents and confronting them is about finding closure with no expectations. Remember that their perception is entirely different from yours. They might not have even perceived their interactions with you to have been traumatic or to have caused you the anxious attachments you currently face. But it is not up to you to get an apology, to get them to see the fault in their ways, or to get them to change. It is a part of you finding your peace and facing the trauma that caused you to deal with anxious attachment styles in your relationship. It takes courage, but remember that you are strong enough to face anything that stands in your path.

Breaking the Cycle

While I have already briefly touched on this concept, it is up to you to break the cycle of trauma and anxious attachments for the generations to come by making sure that you heal yourself entirely and recover from the pain that you have once experienced.

As an individual with anxious attachments, you are not only fixated on the fears and challenges that your relationships pose but also set an example of what you think a relationship should look like. Consider it this way: if you are in a relationship with someone and have kids, you may be so fixated on your past and childhood trauma that you become blinded and oblivious to what happens around you. By virtue of being distracted and focused on your own past and how your parents never met your emotional needs, you also end up being emotionally unavailable to your children and your partner when they might need you. You then continue the cycle of emotional unavailability, and you create the same trauma in your child that your parents created in you.

Additionally, when you express your extreme and irrational feelings of insecurity toward your partner, especially in front of your kids, you set an example for how they should behave in their future relationships. However, your behaviors and emotions are driven by pain and trauma, and this example is not one that you want your kids to follow. This realization then becomes the motivation you need to overcome your own trauma so that you can break the cycle and make sure that your children never have to recover from their experiences as a child.

So how do you break the cycle of trauma, and how do you get the power to disrupt destructive patterns? Well, the first way to do so comes after we have begun our own healing journey we need to understand the importance of the childhood and early developmental years. It is here that we will understand how important childhood experiences are and how critical the early years are. It is here where the blueprint of relationships is formed. By embarking on breaking the cycle, the first thing you do is ensure that the child in your life experiences a different childhood than you did. You break the cycle by altering their experiences.

Because you have experienced trauma, you know exactly what it is that you don't want your child to experience. You then have the power to mold their childhood and experiences so that they experience the nurturing relationship that they deserve and are entitled to. You also get to ensure that you put effort into the relationship with your child so that you are the one they turn to in times of need rather than turning away from you.

Next, you need to consider changing the relationship patterns that you grew up with. This calls for a change in dynamic because you shift your focus away from your experiences of traditional parenting and you move toward parenting in a healthier and safer environment. This undertaking is not easy because as you raise your own children, you, too, are learning a new method of parenting. You are navigating the waters of your parenting journey with no guidance from your own experiences, except that you are certain you don't want to repeat the mistakes of the past.

Then, you need to consider taking as much time and space as needed for you to reflect on your past and assess how far you have come. A part of this journey is changing the relationship you have with yourself. When you give yourself time to reflect on your past in relation to your current situation, you allow yourself to become self-aware in a more acute way, and you get the chance and opportunity to alter your relationships and interactions with those around you.

Finally, remember that the power of breaking the cycle of anxious attachments lies with you. But once you recognize the power you possess, you can learn how to be patient with yourself. Some of what you have experienced can make you frustrated, but when you realize that you need to give yourself time to adjust and recover, you get to face your challenges in a whole new light.

There are moments of extreme courage and resilience that are found when we pursue our journey toward healing. There are moments when we also discover the strength we never knew we had to overcome our challenges. In there, we find our hope for future relationships. While the journey of overcoming anxious attachments isn't an easy one, it helps us build a better version of ourselves. In the next chapter, we are going to look at how you can be the architect of your life, building a better version of yourself.

CHAPTER 6

BUILDING A BETTER SELF

Embracing a new version of yourself is always tricky. How do you navigate the waters of self-discovery? How do you know if this new version of yourself is, in fact, better than the old version? How do you know if you are succeeding at becoming a new version of yourself or if you are so firmly rooted in your ways of old that change seems impossible? These are all valid questions; as you embark on being a better version of yourself, you need to consider just how effective your attempts are.

There are so many things to consider on the journey of self-betterment. While you strive to be a better version of yourself, you also don't want to lose the essence of who you are entirely. This balance is another complexity about how our childhood experiences mold us into who we are.

It is up to us to peel back the layers and intricacies of our lives, to look closely at where our trauma and our identity intersect, and to work toward changing and remedying the parts of ourselves that are broken and bruised without altering the essence of our being.

In this chapter, you are going to learn more about the person who is undeniably closest to you—yourself. You are going to learn about how you can empower yourself through self-discovery, how you can create a better self-awareness in your life, and how you can build healthy boundaries in your life.

Empowering Self-Discovery

Embarking on the complex journey of self-discovery isn't a walk in the park, and it isn't exactly something that occurs naturally. At any given point, we have a firm grasp on our identity; we know who we are because it has been embedded into our DNA. But when we are asked who we actually are, we tend to give scripted answers that we assume cover the basis of who we are. We tend to respond with our name, maybe where we're from, and sometimes what we do for work. But the essence of who we are goes far deeper. It encompasses our dreams and aspirations, which give us motivation in life, help us form our purpose in life, and cultivate our mental, spiritual, and emotional identity.

This topic might seem overwhelming, especially when our autopilot response is so inferior in comparison. But self-discovery involves us asking ourselves difficult questions and actually finding answers to those questions. The only catch is that you shouldn't expect to find answers to such questions immediately but rather understand that self-discovery is a process that often takes time.

According to Elizabeth Perry, a coach on BetterUp who helps clients undergo personal transformations, self-discovery is comprised of three major components *(Perry, 2022)*:

1. **Self-awareness:** This component is where you take the time to look inwardly and get to understand who you are as a person. It is a lot like dating yourself—you learn what your interests are, what your thought processes are, what your feelings are, and why they are so strong in some instances. You will also experience more control over your responses and your thoughts, find yourself experiencing greater empathy, and learn that this knowledge and understanding of yourself provides you with more certainty and confidence in who you are.

2. **Discomfort:** We have already mentioned that this inner work is difficult, but self-discovery also thrusts you into positions that are very uncomfortable. Imagine getting so used to being in one place and one position that the slightest change throws your entire thought process off track. When you discover yourself, you know with certainty who you are, and you can remain consistent despite the inevitable bumps that you may face on the road. But where does this discomfort stem from?

   The discomfort in self-discovery involves facing the trauma and pain you have experienced in your past that undeniably forms a part of who you are but that you have constantly suppressed or avoided because of the pain it causes you. It means facing and correcting the aspects of your life that you would have much rather continued to avoid. It also involves trying new things and getting out of the comfort zone in which no personal development and growth takes place. Try new foods, new activities, and something that you always thought was hard. You might find yourself enjoying something that you always thought you hated, thus progressing your journey of self-discovery.

3. **Intentional living:** This component is self-discovery in practice. Once you know with strong certainty who you are, you become more intentional about how you live every day. You find that your purpose and direction in life are better defined, and you get to align your thoughts, decisions, and emotions with who you are.

Self-discovery matters because it gives you a clear and steadfast way of protecting yourself and tapping into your greatest potential. You see, not only are you able to better interact with people around you because of your confidence, but you are able to set healthy boundaries (which we know are important for healthy relationships and attachments), make confident decisions, treat yourself the way you deserve to be treated, and avoid compromising who you are.

When you know who you are, you know where you are welcomed, and you get to reflect back on the past and identify instances where you weren't treated the way you should have been treated.

Ultimately, this reflection helps you move forward in respecting other people's boundaries because you know how important those boundaries are to you, and you are further able to break the cycle of trauma and toxicity in the relationships you have with others.

Not knowing who you are can plague you with feelings of loneliness. While experiencing an identity crisis isn't something that many of us fully experience, subtle elements of not knowing who you are can creep into your mind and force you to question even the simplest aspects of who you are.

You might even find yourself floating through life without purpose. Despite working hard, you can feel like all you are doing is working to survive and nothing more. Your hopes and dreams might seem futile or unrealistic because the life you are living and practicing doesn't align with the actions you pursue on a daily basis.

What Does Self-Discovery Look Like?

While self-discovery and the intentions behind a self-discovery journey might look different for you when compared to someone else, there are a few common examples that stand out on what the journey actually looks like.

- As you learn more about who you are, you find yourself with a better and unwavering understanding of what your core values are. Life often throws us curveballs when we are faced with situations or decisions that might force us away from what we believe in. But when you have confidence in who you are and what your beliefs are, you find it easier to stand by those beliefs, even if it leaves you as an outsider.

- You know what you want and need, and you won't compromise on your wants and needs. Consider something as simple as being asked what you would like to eat. I have found this one simple question causes a lot of rife in relationships. Many people who have anxious attachments are people-pleasers, and they put the needs and wants of others before their own. This behavior is often a result of their insecurities and their attempts not to want to lose the person they are in a relationship with. Going back to our previous example, they might not want to decide what they want to eat out of fear that their partner might not agree.

- Self-discovery, and the self-awareness that it leads to, help you better identify what your strengths and weaknesses are. You know you can't jump 20 ft in the air because it isn't realistic, and your body wasn't designed to do so. When you know what you are good at, your confidence in those tasks ultimately rises.

- You naturally become more curious and intrigued by the things you either avoided or never considered before. As you become more curious, you begin engaging in activities that you often thought were never something you would do, and as you become more curious, you experience more change. However, with the new-found confidence that you have in yourself, you adapt and accommodate change much easier.

Starting the Journey

Now that we know why self-discovery is so important and all the benefits it can unlock in our lives, you may wonder what the first step actually looks like. Do you need to sit in silence all alone and ask yourself uncomfortable questions? And if so, what questions would you need to ask?

The answer is quite simple. You don't need to separate yourself from the world, and often the first step is as simple as taking note of what your day looks like, what brings you joy, and what brings you irritation. Once you recognize these patterns, you already get to learn a little more about yourself.

But there are other ways for you to begin the journey toward self-discovery, including the following examples:

- journaling
- becoming perceptive of the small and large things in your day
- asking yourself "why" and doing it often
- spending time in prayer or meditation
- trusting your decisions
- failing and learning from that failure
- identifying your passions
- developing healthy and happy habits
- engaging with your inner child
- being kind to yourself
- asking for help when you feel like you aren't making progress

Sometimes, even when you have started your journey of self-discovery, you find yourself going off the rails and falling back into the old habits that you have been consciously trying to break. This is because life moves at a fast pace, and no one stops for you to get to know yourself. As a result, you have to take things into your own hands and make the effort to carve out time for yourself as you embark on this journey.

As you succeed in discovering who you truly are, you find that this knowledge of yourself trickles down into other facets of your life. You will find your relationships becoming stronger, you will be more confident, you will be kinder and not so hard on yourself, you'll tap into creativity veins that you never knew existed before, and you will find that your focus and determination are more honed in *(Perry, 2022a)*.

Once you find yourself firmly rooted in the ongoing journey of self-discovery, you will also find yourself recognizing and confronting the subtle negative thoughts that you never knew you so consistently had. You see, as you set the bar for yourself on how you expect others to treat you, you also start learning how you need to treat yourself. You realize that your negative thoughts are not something you would say to those closest to you, and you start questioning why you are saying them to yourself.

You get the opportunity to confront the negative thoughts that you have become so accustomed to hearing, and you learn to reframe your thoughts. Becoming self-aware allows you to change the perceptions you once had of yourself. Instead of criticizing your weaknesses, you find yourself acknowledging and accepting them and focusing more on your strengths.

As you learn who you are, you not only empower yourself, but your self-awareness helps you better identify what your triggers are in your anxious attachment patterns.

Developing Self-Awareness

Every component of who we are comes with good and bad, or at least what we perceive as good and bad. Yes, the purpose of self-discovery is to learn who you are and to share the positivity and confidence of who you are with everyone else, but it is also about tapping into your past and the traumas that caused you to develop anxious attachment patterns.

Remember that anxious attachments can even exist within ourselves. We find ourselves unhealthily attached to certain parts of ourselves or habits that ultimately lead to our downfall, but we just can't seem to shake them. Being self-aware means that you recognize your own anxious attachment patterns within your relationships, and you work toward confronting and overcoming them.

It isn't as simple as identifying your patterns which could be insecurity, difficulties in trusting your partner, or even the constant need for reassurance in your relationship. Instead, it means learning these patterns and then working your way backward into understanding and knowing what triggered these patterns.

EMILY JOHNSON

When we get sick, we are sometimes told that all we can do is treat the symptoms of our illness rather than directly treat the illness. However, identifying our triggers is the exact opposite. Instead of just managing our responses to a trigger or dealing with the effects of our anxious attachments, we come face-to-face with the thing that has caused us to feel anxious.

No two people experience the same trigger. Sometimes it is even difficult to recognize how a trigger can elicit a certain emotional response from you because the two just seem so vastly unrelated. While there are a few common triggers that may set someone off, most of us have unique triggers that have become a source of derision in our own lives.

Some of the more common triggers that can make you feel emotionally uneasy or that cause your anxious attachment patterns to blow out of proportion include being lied to, being treated unfairly, experiencing rejection or betrayal, suddenly having your beliefs challenged, being ignored, or being irrationally and rudely criticized.

When you become self-aware, you realize what your triggers are because you become more attuned to your mind, your body, the sensations you experience, and the emotions you feel. When you have experienced a trigger, your body lets you know that it is experiencing a negative shift in its emotional responses. You may find that someone does or says something, and suddenly, you are experiencing all the sensations of anxiety: your heart is racing, you are sweating, your breathing has increased, and you may feel weak in your legs. This anxious response usually means that you have experienced a trigger *(Raypole, 2020)*.

As soon as you have become attuned to the sensations caused by the trigger, you can immediately backtrack and identify exactly what it was that caused these feelings, thus identifying your trigger.

Once you have identified the trigger, whether it was an internal thought in your mind or an external experience, it is up to you to control your response to these triggers. You can either let your trigger control you and evoke the response that is unsettling to you, or you could take the following three steps:

1. Acknowledge your feelings instead of burying them. When you face your feelings, you show yourself that despite the emotions and anxiety you experience, you still are able to control the way you respond and interact with others. Still, you pause and process your thoughts before engaging, and that gives you control over your triggers rather than giving your triggers control over you.

2. Put some physical distance between you and the triggering situation. In most cases, you aren't able to control or manipulate the situation, but you can remove yourself from something that is triggering to you. Giving yourself space allows you to calm the heavy breathing, the racing heart, and the sweaty palms, and it allows you to gain control over yourself. It also allows you to rationalize and engage with your triggering moment

while safely being removed from it. In this way, you can use coping mechanisms such as breathing exercises or mindfulness to calm yourself down.

3. Communicate with the person that is triggering you. As previously mentioned, sometimes our triggers stem from intrusive thoughts, but many times, they stem from the actions or words of another person. In these cases, we can't control what the other person does or does not say and do; we can only control the way we interact and respond to them. Communicate your triggers with the person but do it in a way where you focus on using I statements which show them that it is your responses to their words and actions instead of accusing them of something that they are quite accustomed to doing.

I once had a client come in and was absolutely distraught by the behavior of her fiancé and his family members at a Thanksgiving dinner. She came in crying and was utterly broken by what had happened. As we delved into the situation, it turned out that her fiancé and his family members affectionately tease and joke with each other around the dinner table. This was all good fun, and my client admitted that when it was directed at other people, it did elicit quite a few laughs from her. However, as the night progressed, she had her turn of being teased.

But my client was raised in a home where eating together, let alone speaking to each other, wasn't a norm. Further, she was verbally and emotionally abused by her mother and had an absent father. When she became the subject of the lighthearted joking, she couldn't help but take it personally, and she couldn't understand why her partner joined in with the teasing instead of protecting her.

We learned that her trigger was what she perceived as verbal abuse. This was highlighted when we tapped into the trauma of her past and when we explored the interactions that stood out most in her mind between her parents and herself. When we had a couple's session with her partner, we were able to work through her triggers, and we were able to overcome the very thing that stood in the way of her fully integrating with his family. This was done by them first overtly stating their intentions. She needed to understand that her fiancé didn't have any ill intentions toward her, and he needed to understand that what he found humorous was hurtful to her. Through communication and by placing themselves in vulnerable positions with each other, they were able to move past the sensitive issues in their relationship.

As you come face-to-face with your triggers, you will also find yourself becoming more aware and more mindful of your interactions, the people you surround yourself with, and the places you go. You will find that as you're processing your way through your anxious attachments, you may not engage with your parents in the same way because you can identify a triggering situation before you are thrust into the discomfort that it ultimately brings with it.

Building Healthy Boundaries

Boundaries are established by identifying the own line in your life that you choose not to compromise on. When you establish boundaries, you show people where they are safe to reside in your life, and you show them what areas and beliefs are not compromisable. You show people where they are allowed to meet you in the space of your life, and you show them at what point you are willing to come for them.

Anything that resides out of or beyond your boundaries needs to be inaccessible. This concept also means that you need to make sure that you don't leave the safety of your boundaries to meet someone in their place of comfort.

If you or someone you know exhibits anxious attachment patterns, the truth is that they are someone who desperately needs boundaries. The boundaries will not only protect them, but they will also allow other people in their lives not to overstep.

But what are boundaries, and how do you establish them in a healthy way? Boundaries are a way of taking care of your mental, emotional, spiritual, and physical health. Your boundaries allow others to see what is permissible in terms of who you are as a person and what should not even be considered.

Boundaries are rigid, they are not flexible, and the second they become flexible or optional is when your boundaries wither away. But it is important to remember that we will likely set different boundaries with different people. The boundaries we establish with acquaintances will be different from the ones we establish with close friends, and those will be different from the boundaries we establish with our family members or our romantic partners.

Additionally, it also serves us well to remember that other people also have boundaries, and we need to respect those boundaries. Often their boundaries won't look anything like ours. And if you find that someone's boundaries are not compatible with your own, the best way to keep both of you safe is to walk away from the relationship.

Now comes the hard part, which is setting and establishing boundaries with people. This step might be especially difficult to do, especially with your parents and with people you have known even before you began confronting and facing your anxious attachments. But setting boundaries can be done quite simply *(Boundaries: What Are They and How to Create Them, 2022)*:

1. First, you need to acknowledge that you are deserving of the boundaries you are going to set. You deserve to be treated correctly, and you need to establish the benchmark that others need to adhere to.

2. Then you need to establish your boundaries with yourself. Know what it is that you are and aren't willing to accept from someone, understand what it is you are going to be firm about, and how you are going to enforce and reinforce your firmness.

3. And finally, you need to communicate your boundaries with the people in your life. No one is going to know that you have established boundaries unless you tell them. Be open and be honest and be comfortable enough and at

ease to know that if they don't respect your boundaries, they probably shouldn't be in your life.

Once your boundaries have been established and communicated, you are going to need to continuously enforce them and sometimes remind those around you of them. Eventually, those who respect you and your boundaries will never overstep the boundaries because they associate your boundaries so strongly with your presence.

Boundaries can look like politely declining an invite to go somewhere, it can look like saying no, it can be you expressing your pleasure or displeasure about something, it can look like you engaging with someone directly and talking to them directly about your feelings, and it can look like you making your feelings and thoughts known.

There are often instances where we leave our boundaries unspoken, and we expect those around us to guess what we are feeling or when they have overstepped and made us feel uncomfortable. Instead, when you are open about your boundaries, you make it known and clear that you are confident enough to share these boundaries. In the same way, if our relationship changes and our boundaries change with a person, we need to communicate these changes with them too.

Relationships are fluid and change often. If a friend turns into a romantic partner, the boundaries will change, as they should. Just in the same way, someone who we were once close with or had a close relationship with is no longer someone we go to in our times of need and is someone from whom we have drifted apart. In those instances, your boundaries also need to be communicated and asserted. While it may be uncomfortable to let someone who used to be close to you know that you have established new boundaries so that you can protect yourself from the anxiety they cause in your life, it needs to be done.

Communicating your boundaries is usually where situations get slightly more complicated. We think that we are effectively communicating when we really aren't. A lot of the time, our boundaries can come off as accusations when we tell people that they are wrong for overstepping our boundaries. It can even sound accusatory when we tell them that we are establishing boundaries to protect ourselves from whatever they might have done in the past to hurt us. Instead, we need to consider that not everyone is on the journey that we are on, and a lot of the time, people aren't intentional about their interactions and words. In most cases, they don't even realize that they have caused us hurt and pain. But we can only focus on our emotional responses to their actions and not on the intentions behind their words and actions.

When you communicate, it is important to be clear, open, and honest about what you are feeling and experiencing. It is also good to attach a "why" to everything you feel. Explain where your feelings stem from, and be as honest as you can. With effective communication, it is important to make explicitly clear everything you hope to communicate with someone and leave no ambiguity or anything up to the imagination. Stunted or ineffective communication often comes when we leave people to fill in the blanks about our feelings. This behavior is not reasonable, nor is it fair, since there is far too much space for misinterpretation or ignored feelings.

While communication is extremely important, there are also other facets that need to be considered. Imagine you're sitting in a crowded family-style restaurant that is bustling and busy; children are running around and playing, and there is jovial laughter going on all around you. This setting would not be ideal for communicating boundaries or trauma with your partner.

Instead, there are ways that you can be open and honest, even about the difficult aspects of a relationship, if you communicate in the correct way. This process starts with choosing the right time and place to communicate. We all know the dreaded words of someone telling you they need to talk to you. So instead of giving your partner or anyone else in your life a heart attack and anxiety, it is always best to communicate in a space where you are both safe, calm, and quiet, and when you both have time to start and end a conversation successfully.

It is also important to remember that communication is not one-sided. If you are going to be engaging with your partner or family member, you also need to allow them the opportunity to respond to whatever it is that you are saying. You need to take the time to listen to what they need to say as they have done with you. You also need to consider that if you are communicating boundaries, you have probably been thinking about them for a while. Your mind has had the time to process and understand its reasoning and feelings, but now you need to give the other person the time to process and understand their reactions and feelings to what you have said. Sometimes, effective communication means giving the other person time to process their feelings. Once they have taken time to process and understand their feelings, they can come back to you for you both to discuss matters even further.

And finally, remember that you are not entitled to anyone's ear. This means that someone can choose to listen to you or not, and in turn, you can choose who you listen to. When someone does pay attention and listens to what it is you are communicating, it is important for you to thank them for giving you their time and attention.

As I have gone down the healing journey with many of my clients, I have seen several of them finding themselves and rebuilding themselves by establishing boundaries. They found their confidence when they learned that they were worthy of more than they were receiving. Most people don't realize just how much they are deserving of it until they set boundaries and find that people actually respect their boundaries.

In the next chapter, we are going to look at how you can embrace secure connections fully now that you have ventured down your path of healing. We are going to look at how you can embrace this aspect of life and move forward in relationships in a way that is full of confidence and peace. You will be equipped with the tools you need to be a person who is securely attached to others.

CHAPTER 7

EMBRACING SECURE ATTACHMENT

We all want to be treated a certain way; we want to be loved, respected, and appreciated. Sometimes, if we are unfamiliar with those feelings, we may not recognize them or appreciate them when we do experience them. It seems strange to be around people who love and appreciate us. This is the heartbreaking reality of the people who don't readily have loving people around them.

However, learning to embrace the love and affection that comes from a secure relationship is extremely important. For those who grew up in a home where they were faced with anxious attachments, embracing secure attachments can be difficult. Because they become so untrusting of people, they tend to question the intentions of those with whom they are in a relationship.

The importance of secure attachments starts at the point of establishment. This means that from childhood, secure attachments need to be established so that the child can grow into an adult who forms healthy and happy relationships. However, those adults who have experienced anxious attachments in the formative years can often remedy their attachment styles in their adulthood.

Secure attachments are important because they teach your young baby very important habits about bonds and the relationships they will ultimately form. When a parent is always there for a child, they teach the child to have trust in the parent's presence. There is a surety that no matter what the circumstances are, their parent will always be there for them. However, we don't mean in an unhealthy way or in a way that takes independence away from a child. Instead, the parent shows the child that they will be there to teach them, support them, and assist them, should assistance ever be required. This behavior teaches the child to be confident on their own while having the security of knowing that their parent is never too far out of reach.

Additionally, the importance of secure attachments forms the foundation of healthy relationships. With young children, having a secure bond with their parents teaches them that they can trust their parents, they can communicate all their emotions with their parents in a safe way, and they can trust others around them as well *(Robinson et al., n.d.).*

As newer generations of parents try to break the toxic cycles that they grew up with, they find themselves questioning the traditional parenting methods that they were raised with. They are told by their parents and older generations that carrying their child, being there for their child, giving their child all of their attention, and catering to their child's basic needs means they're spoiling them. And they often use the notion or idea of being spoiled as something that is entirely negative.

Young parents have made a concerted effort to avoid these negative notions around parenting, especially once they realize that showing their child acts of love and kindness does not constitute the negative idea of being spoiled. Children deserve to be loved, they deserve to receive attention from their parents, and they are entitled to affection and respect. This thought process is why so many people from this generation have faced trauma. However, they are also acutely aware that they have been raised in a way that stunted the connections and bonds that they form with people. As a result, they are more attuned to creating and establishing secure attachments with their child.

Parents today realize the importance of developing secure attachments with their children. They have a better understanding of the impact secure attachments will have on their overall emotional and relational health and know how greatly it will affect their mental well-being.

It is important to remember that raising your child with secure attachments doesn't mean that you have prevented them from experiencing any trauma. Instead, it means that you have equipped them with the emotional and mental tools that will help them handle, process, and overcome the trauma that they will inevitably face through the course of their life.

Additionally, it raises them to have strong willpower, confidence, and high enough self-esteem so that they can overcome any challenges that might come their way. It teaches them how to be resilient and face life's challenges with the knowledge of overcoming the difficulties in life rather than just allowing themselves to experience the vicissitudes of life. Ultimately, you want to equip the child with the ability to overcome life's challenges rather than just allowing life to have its way with them.

I had many clients come to me feeling like they were buckling under the pressure of life. They often felt overwhelmed and that their struggles were exponentially greater than the trouble and problems of those around them. As we discussed their feelings, the discussion inevitably pivoted toward attachment styles, and it was found that they were ill-equipped to handle the difficulties that life threw at them. The reason why their difficulties seemed magnified in comparison to those around them was that other people had better coping mechanisms for life's difficulties, and they were left battered and bruised by their problems. Instead of facing their problems and finding a resolution to the issues of life, they try to hide from their problems or avoid them altogether.

Through our therapy sessions, we worked through some realities of life, one of which was that no one is exempt from struggles. The only difference is that some people are better equipped to manage and handle their struggles. This difficulty is equipping an adult with the emotional and mental tools they should have developed as a young child. However, developing these tools is possible as long as you put in the time and effort.

Establishing secure attachments in your children at a young age is important because it also helps them foster healthy relationships in their adult relationships.

Tools for Nurturing Secure Attachments

We know that in early childhood, developing secure attachments is dependent on the parent and the parent's interactions with the child. This means that nurturing secure attachments in childhood is easier to do. This work can be done by ensuring that you are mindfully present and available to your child. Catering to your child's needs, practicing active listening, and providing emotional support are ways of ensuring that they develop secure attachments.

If you feel like you are failing your child or you just aren't certain if you are creating a secure attachment, you could begin implementing these steps *(Herr, 2015)*:

- Embrace and cuddle with your baby often. It has been well established that skin-to-skin contact between a parent and a child is extremely important *(Skin-To-Skin Contact, 2023)*. From the newborn age, parents are encouraged to spend time bonding with their baby by engaging in skin-to-skin contact. But this practice shouldn't stop after the newborn stage. Embrace and cuddle with your child often and for as long as possible.

You show them that you are physically there for them, and it has a major calming effect on them and on you.

- Make as much eye contact with your baby as possible. I know this may seem weird because when we engage with someone and make eye contact, we hope for some level of understanding. However, while your child may not directly understand you, engaging in eye contact ensures that you form a strong bond with them from a very young age. It also establishes the level of attention you should be giving your child. Every time you engage with them, you will immediately be compelled to make eye contact with them, and this, in turn, will set a benchmark for them to expect people to look at them in the eye when they are engaging with them.

- Listen to your baby and become attuned to their needs. As a parent, you are naturally inclined to focus on your baby's cues. This level of focus is something that needs to continue as they grow. As a parent, you need to know when your child is feeling down or despondent. If they are unnaturally quiet, or if they seem to be closed off, you need to be aware so that you can provide them with the support they need, even if they aren't asking for it outright.

- Be fully present and fully involved with your child. When you engage and communicate with them, try not to be distracted. Learning how to be fully present and mindful of each moment you spend with your child is extremely important. We often try to multitask or be productive when we are with our kids, but as soon as we focus on just being with our children and doing nothing else, we find that our relationship with them elevates entirely.

As an adult, nurturing secure attachments looks quite different. You see, when you engage with your child, you establish secure attachments, and they will grow up with these attachment styles. However, as an adult, you are learning for the first time what most children begin learning as an infant. By this point in your life, you have been hurt, you have experienced emotional difficulties, and you have faced the inevitable challenges that many experience in life.

As an adult, it begins with the relationship we have with ourselves. We need to care for and nurture the bond we are forming with ourselves. Once you can find a safe space within yourself and your own mind, and once you show yourself that you, too, are trustworthy, you can work on your relationships and bonds with either person.

Once you set the benchmark with yourself and establish a healthy relationship with yourself, you can then compare the other relationships that you have in your life with the relationship you have with yourself. If those relationships do not live up to the standard you have begun developing with yourself, you need to work toward distancing yourself from those people.

Eventually, you can begin working on expressing your emotions in a better and healthier way, and begin building up your self-esteem and self-awareness. It is a starting point for you to begin the journey of developing a better relationship with yourself and with others. The reality is that some people need to start their journey later in life. But this doesn't mean that they are doomed to suffer with their attachment style forever. They can always work toward bettering themselves and their emotional health.

Tools for Transformation

There is a unique concept of emotional resilience that exists, which many expect to mean that you are immune to stresses and difficulties. However, emotional resilience means that you are able to face stresses and difficulties without it entirely derailing the trajectory of your life.

Emotional resilience is not about you winning the battles that you face emotionally, but rather how you get through the difficult moments and come out on the other side. Let us consider two examples: I have a client who, at the earliest sign of strife and difficulty, immediately finds themself drawn to alcohol. They don't know how to face difficulties and stress, and they find it almost impossible to sort through the many ideas, thoughts, and feelings that are running through their mind. They would find themselves crippled by anxiety when a situation deviated from the expected plan. In their work environment, challenges were bound to arise, and they were obviously in an environment where alcohol was inaccessible. This situation would often lead to them becoming frantic and on the verge of a panic attack or mental breakdown.

On the other hand, I had a client who always seemed to be level-headed. Despite not being immune to the difficulties and the stresses that life throws our way, they were able to work through their difficulties, and they were able to take the time to process and decompress after extremely stressful or emotionally disturbing situations. Many people looked at them with concern wondering if they felt any emotions, but the most common question they were asked was, "How do you handle difficulties so well?" The truth was that they were equipped to face the difficulties of life with confidence and with the understanding that their circumstances were not a reflection of their difficulties.

The way we can develop emotional resilience is by understanding the three facets that are involved in our responses to emotional distress. The first facet is our thought process and the way our mind processes what is occurring. The second facet is our perception which is how we assess and understand the situation. Finally, the third facet involves our actions and how we respond to what we have experienced *(Chowdhury, 2019)*.

Once we understand how the three above elements intertwine with each other, we realize that our thoughts affect our actions. In other words, our minds ultimately determine the way we respond to stress. This leads us to work on ourselves first internally so that we can respond better externally.

How do you develop better emotional resilience? It isn't going to be an overnight process where suddenly you are harder and have a don't-care attitude. No, it means building up your emotions so that while you do feel the stresses and difficulties of life, you know how to work through and overcome them. It means establishing boundaries and steering clear of situations that are likely to make you feel stressed.

However, emotional resilience is an internal process. It is about finding balance internally and becoming in tune with yourself. Remember, the goal isn't to stop feeling your emotions but rather to better regulate and manage them.

So what does the internal process of emotional regulation look like? It closely involves being self-aware. This concept has been a theme throughout this book because it is important. When you are self-aware, you are able to recognize extreme emotions and extreme emotional responses to external stimuli. Next, it comes with you changing your own perception of yourself. We all tend to be extremely hard on ourselves, and we expect more from ourselves than we do from others. However, this mindset can be changed and adapted when you realize that no one is perfect. You allow yourself some room to make mistakes, allowing your emotions to better handle whatever it is you are dealing with.

With self-awareness comes the ability to notice and identify when you are feeling emotionally drained. You may be feeling tired, overwhelmed, or like everything around you is one second away from setting you off. It is in this situation that you need to allow yourself time to step away so that you can better manage your emotions and calm your feelings down. This might look like engaging in self-care, allowing yourself to rest for a while, and spending time with people who emotionally support you.

When you develop emotional resilience, you are better able to engage in relationships. You find yourself having a better bond with those around you because you control your emotions instead of allowing your emotions to control you. This means that in a disagreement or an emotionally heated situation, you are better able to respond to the situation instead of exploding and causing your emotions to cause derision in a situation.

As people have worked through the process of overcoming their anxious attachments, they have found themselves more at ease in their own skin and in their relationships. They have found the confidence in themselves to walk away from situations where they feel unwanted, and they have found themselves engaging with people in the same way that they want to be treated. This means they learned to fill the space in their environment.

In relationships, overcoming their anxious attachments looked a lot like being comfortable, no longer plagued by the discomfort of insecurities. They transitioned from their insecurities and fear that that their partner would abandon them to being comfortable and learning to trust. This does not mean that overcoming your attachment styles means that your relationship will immediately become successful. Instead, it means that even if your relationship fails, you have the emotional resilience to overcome the heartbreak without blaming future partners for the hurt of the past.

People who overcome anxious attachments find themselves with a newfound sense of security and emotional stability. This emotional stability is sustained and maintained even if they are in relationships with people who have insecure attachments. In fact, I have found that people who have overcome their anxious attachments actually serve as a good example to those who are still on their journey toward overcoming their anxious attachments. I find that they tend to get into relationships with people who do have anxious attachments, and in many instances, they work together as a couple to overcome their anxious attachments.

The success stories that come from overcoming anxious attachments usually mean that someone has found emotional stability in their life. They have found a safe space in being themselves and a safe space in their relationships.

Overcoming anxious attachments isn't just about overcoming and fighting through the battles we face in our heads. Rather, it is about becoming a better person, a stronger person, and someone who serves as a strong rock in their relationships. Changing your attachment styles means that you are now someone who is the pillar of strength in their relationship. But it goes even further than that. It means that you are now someone who will raise their kids with secure attachments, and that means that you are already breaking generational cycles of trauma.

As someone who has overcome their insecure attachments, you become a better and stronger person. You become someone who is well-rounded and who can better respond and interact with the difficulties that life poses to you.

In the next chapter, we are going to take a closer look at the success stories of the people who have overcome their anxious attachments. We are going to look at how they become better and stronger individuals, and we are going to see how their relationships benefitted from the change and how they became happier people in their relationships.

The change you will make is not temporary, it is a permanent one that will benefit every relationship you form in your life.

CHAPTER 8

ENDING WITH SUCCESS

The transformation of anyone moving from anxious attachments to secure attachments is truly phenomenal. It is a success story that deserves to be shared and needs to be told so that others can see just how possible this change and transition actually is.

One of the most notable success stories that stands out for me is the story of a client who faced extreme abuse in her childhood. She was often left to fend for herself, and as someone who faced abandonment at home, the last thing they needed was to face abandonment at school or within the social aspects of their lives. And yet, she was dealt the unfortunate hand of attending school and being severely bullied because she so often isolated herself.

She was a victim by all accounts. However, at the time, she didn't realize that there was a source and a reason behind her difficulties. As she grew older, she began getting involved in romantic relationships, which unfortunately looked a lot like the relationships her mother had with her father. Her partners would physically, emotionally, and mentally abuse her, but because she was so desperate for their love, she would endure and stay in the relationship, thinking that she was showing them unconditional love. However, the only person that truly suffered was her.

After having multiple failed relationships, she realized that she did not want to continue facing a world that hurt her and constantly took away from her rather than feeding into her. She took matters into her own hands and came to me to seek help.

As with all of my clients, we started at the very beginning. It was here where we found the patterns of trauma and abuse that existed and that were formed at a very young age in her life. We uncovered how her relationship with her parents developed and how she would have liked them to change. But the most profound thing that I found in my sessions with her was the motivation behind why she wanted to change these disruptive patterns in her life. She knew and identified that something was wrong in her life; she found that she was deeply dissatisfied with parts of her life, and the only way she could change it and gain control of her life was by starting with herself.

She shared with me that her motivation was that she desperately wanted children, but she never wanted her children to grow up with the same issues that she faced. It is for this reason, dear reader, that I have greatly emphasized the importance of breaking

ANXIOUS ATTACHMENT RECOVERY

cycles because that is what I have found to motivate so many on their journey toward developing secure attachments.

By working on the relationship she had with herself, engaging with her feelings, and becoming more self-aware, she was able to develop secure attachments. The moment in which I knew we had a breakthrough was the day I received an invite to her wedding. She had found someone with whom she could openly communicate, who was always there for her, and who helped her overcome her anxious attachments. Today, they have three beautiful kids, all of whom have secure attachments because their parents were always there for them, always cared for them, and always catered to their needs.

I have also encountered people who developed renewed relationships with people that they were already in a relationship with, but their relationship was strained by their anxious attachments. However, they worked on themselves both individually and as a couple so that they could overcome the difficulties and the strain that was placed on their relationship.

Working together to overcome anxious attachments made them realize just how much potential their relationships had. I have watched couples go from being on the verge of divorce or separation to entirely overcoming their challenges and coming out on the other side with renewed love and a stronger relationship.

Although our attachment styles are formed and based on the bonds and relationships we have with other people, the only way for us to heal from the scars our attachments have left behind is by healing from within. It can feel like it is something you are doing alone, and the journey can feel long. But as you venture down your path toward healing, you learn that the reason why it seems lonely is because you are the only one facing your own unique traumas. This, however, doesn't mean that you can't find the support that you need. and deserve.

Once you have begun establishing boundaries, you find that there are people who are willing to stick by you as you heal. Those are the people who will support you in your difficult times, and those are the people you should surround yourself with.

Finding Your Own Success

While I can share endless success stories with you, I often find people comparing the rate of healing with others. But one thing is for certain: healing does not happen at the same time for everyone. Everyone's journey is their own and is unique. You cannot measure the success of your healing journey based on someone else. The trauma that you experience is different from that of someone else. So, while success stories are here to motivate you and to help you see the light at the end of the tunnel, it is also not a benchmark for you to use to measure your healing.

Healing is not a finite or measurable aspect of life. One day, you wake up, and you realize that what once triggered you before, or what was once a source of infinite pain, suddenly hurts slightly less. You don't feel battered and bruised, and the crippling anxiety you once felt has seemed to vanish. You find that you are no longer afraid or insecure in your relationships, you find yourself being more trusting, and you realize that while you are in a relationship, you are still both individuals, which means you have no reason to cling to your partner to overwhelming extents.

As you embark on your own healing journey, remember while you are the person who will benefit most from overcoming your trauma and anxiety, you also serve as a beacon of hope for your children and for the generations that come after your children. But your legacy doesn't just end there. Instead, your story will also serve as a beacon of hope for strangers, people whom you have never met, who are also looking for a promise that no matter how long it takes, everything will get better. They want to know that they can overcome the anxiety that plagues their relationships, and they want to know that they can overcome their triggers.

This is where the joy and beauty of life lie, and the best part is that it is within reach. Your healing is within your grasp, and you will find yourself growing as an individual and as a pair.

There is always hope for a renewed life and for fulfilling relationships. There is always a way for you to find the bonds you have so desperately yearned for, but it all starts with healing yourself and nurturing the accumulated wounds.

There are different scenarios that you may find yourself in when you are on the path toward healing. You might find yourself in a relationship, recovering from a failed relationship, entering into a new relationship, or just focusing on yourself. I often tell my clients that the best time for them to find healing is to be by themselves. However, I will never encourage a couple to break their relationship. That is why, as much as this journey is your own, I always recommend that the healing is done with your partner.

The healing you find not only gives you a world of good but also allows your partner and your children to experience the life you've always dreamed of—a life free of trauma, hurt, and toxicity!

CONCLUSION

Dear reader, you have made your way to the end of this book. It is with sincere hope that you have been equipped with the tools you need to establish healthier bonds and connections with those around you.

The reason and motivation behind this book was to create a society of people who know their worth and who are able to form human connections the way they were meant to be formed. We need to embrace each other and embrace the connections we have with each other. Life is too short to be surrounded by people who hurt you and who cause you dissatisfaction and hurt. Instead, it is through this book that I hoped to encourage people to heal themselves so that they can experience bonds in the beautiful way it was intended to be.

Through the course of this book, you will have learned all about the different attachment styles that exist. Through this understanding, you will be equipped to better recognize and understand these attachments in yourself and in the bonds you form with those around you. I also firmly believe that if you know how certain attachment styles originate, you have the power to control these attachments in your life.

Next, we have looked at anxious attachment. Specific to this book, we have focused on anxious attachments and how these form in people's lives. We have seen the relationship and bond between parent and child that would have cultivated an anxious attachment in the child. By understanding the relationship dynamics that lead to anxious attachments, we know what actions would prevent such attachments from forming. Knowing what to avoid is a sure way of ensuring that anxious attachments are eradicated in your own life, with your children, and for generations to come.

Beyond just gaining an understanding and insight into anxious attachments, we have also learned how this attachment style can seep into different facets of your life and how it can affect your day-to-day living. Anxious attachments influence all relationships and bonds that we form. And while we see its effects most prominently in our romantic relationships, it will ultimately also influence how we handle stress in our workplace and how we engage with our colleagues as well.

We have then learned how you can overcome anxious attachments. We have seen the steps that you can take as an individual toward first healing yourself and then equipping yourself with the tools that you need to form healthier connections in your relationships. We have seen that this will not only benefit the future relationships you will form but also the current relationships you find yourself in.

ANXIOUS ATTACHMENT RECOVERY

As you heal your mind and heart from the trauma that you experienced from your anxious attachments, we have learned how you can use these tools to become a better version of yourself. Remember, you are not becoming a better version of yourself for other people, but rather, you are doing it for yourself. You are becoming a version of yourself that your mind and heart deserve.

Becoming someone who forms secure attachments is not just good for your own mental and emotional health, but it is also good for future generations to come. If you are someone who ultimately breaks the cycle of anxious attachments in your life, you become the person who sets an example for your children on what healthy relationships look like and what they should expect from a relationship. We set the benchmark for our relationships, we choose how we allow people to treat us and engage with us. Breaking the cycle of anxious attachments shows your children that they deserve to be treated with love and care.

While it is hard to set and accept the high standards that come with secure attachments, embracing security in your life sets the tone for your destiny and the life you are meant to live. We all need to be loved in a way that doesn't cause fear or anxiety. We should never have to face relationships that feel like we are falling under the burden of anxiety. We should never be in relationships that cause us to feel fear, and most importantly, our minds shouldn't be the tool that is used against us in our relationships.

Of everything you have learned in the book, dear reader, my greatest hope is that you have learned that change is possible. My greatest hope is that you will have read this book's success stories and seen yourself in those stories. Everyone can come out on the other end; all it takes is for you to work on yourself.

Remember that it is important to embrace healthy connections for you to achieve healing and growth in your relationships. By doing so, you get to experience love and a stronger bond in your relationships, which is exactly the way relationships were meant to be. Remember that your relationship is meant to be a safe place. The world is already a hard and difficult place. On its own, the world has enough anxiety to give. Because we face so much anxiety in the world, our relationship is meant to be somewhere we can go for peace and happiness, not somewhere where there is more strife and difficulties. That is what we deserve from our relationships.

It is also important to consider that this journey is not going to be easy. It is going to be challenging, and you are going to be confronted with parts of your past that you might rather forget. However, you will learn something profound about yourself. You will learn that you are strong enough to overcome the barriers that once stood in the way of you forming healthy relationships. You have the power to embrace the change and find fulfilling relationships.

It is now time for you to take the first step toward self-awareness, self-discovery, and transformation. The first step of this journey is the hardest, but it sets the rest of your life on a trajectory of calmness and peace. You have the ability to overcome anxious attachments and find love and fulfillment in your life once again.

With this newfound strength and the confidence that will ultimately come from your journey of healing, it is time to venture forth with courage. It is time to make your connections powerful and valuable, and it is time to treasure yourself.

As you embark on this journey of self-discovery, never forget that you deserve the highest level of love possible. Also, remember that the strongest form of love you will ever experience is self-love. Love yourself first and show others the way you deserve to be loved and treated. Set the tone for the rest of your life and make sure that you never settle for less because you truly do deserve the best life has to offer.

Now, let us go forth and build strong relationships—relationships that our children can admire one day!

THANK YOU

Thank you for reading *Anxious Attachment Recovery* through to the end. I hope the book has proved to be valuable on your journey of self-discovery and having better relationships.

Any feedback or suggestions you have would contribute tremendously in helping me improve my writing and make the book better. Please do not hesitate to share your thoughts with me by leaving a review on the Amazon book page. You can do so by scanning the QR code below, which will lead you to the review page:

Sincerely,
Emily

REFERENCES

Ackerman, C. E. (2018, May 23). *What is self-esteem? A psychologist explains.* Positive Psychology. https://positivepsychology.com/self-esteem/ #:~:text=Various%20factors%20believed%20to%20influence

Addressing childhood trauma as an adult. (2020, July 13). Viva Center. https://www.vivapartnership.com/happenings/addressing-childhood-trauma-as-an-adult/

American Psychological Association. (2021). Trauma and shock. *American Psychological Association.* https://www.apa.org/topics/trauma

Anwar, B. (2023, January 27). Self-Sabotaging relationships: Signs & causes. *Talkspace.* https://www.talkspace.com/blog/self-sabotaging-relationship/

Bermudez, V. (2021, May 10). *Parental preference - babies.* Bella Luna Family. https://bellalunafamily.com/parental-preference-babies/#:~:text=These%20feelings%20are%20normal%20and

BetterHelp. (2023, July 3). *What is withdrawn behavior and what causes it?* BetterHelp. https://www.betterhelp.com/advice/behavior/what-is-withdrawn-behavior-and-what-causes-it/

Beyer, A. L. (2020, September 24). *Do your relationships often seem to self-destruct? Figure out if you're the one who's been setting the clock*. Greatist. https://greatist.com/grow/relationship-self-sabotage#:~:text=Relationship%20wreckers%20like%20 cheating%2C%20lying

Bose, J. (2020, June 12). *Importance of secure attachment*. DadPad. https://thedadpad.co.uk/mental-health/infant-mental-health-the-importance-of-secure-attachment/#:~:text=Although%20 no%20guarantee%20of%20lifelong

Boundaries: What are they and how to create them. (2022, February 25). Wellness Center University of Illinois Chicago. https:// wellnesscenter.uic.edu/news-stories/boundaries-what-are-they-and-how-to-create-them/#:~:text=Setting%20 boundaries%20is%20a%20form

Brennan, D. (2021, April 8). *What is anxious attachment?* WebMD. https://www.webmd.com/mental-health/ what-is-anxious-attachment

Cafasso, J. (2019, November 14). *Anxious attachment: Signs in children and adults, causes, and more*. Healthline. https://www.healthline.com/health/mental-health/ anxious-attachment#causes

Cherry, K. (2023a, February 22). *What is attachment theory?* Verywell Mind. https://www.verywellmind.com/ what-is-attachment-theory-2795337

Cherry, K. (2023b, June 30). *What causes social withdrawal?* Verywell Mind. https://www.verywellmind.com/what-causes-social-withdrawal-7095469#:~:text=Signs%20of%20 Social%20Withdrawal&text=Some%20examples%20of%20 social%20withdrawal

Chowdhury, M. R. (2019, January 22). *What is emotional resilience and how to build it? (+Training exercises)*. PositivePsychology. https://positivepsychology.com/emotional-resilience/

Darcy, A. M. (2016, August 16). *Fear of abandonment - 12 signs it is secretly sabotaging your relationships*. Harley Therapy Blog. https://www.harleytherapy.co.uk/counselling/fear-of-abandonment.htm#:~:text=Fear%20of%20abandonment%20can%20mean

Davis, N. (n.d.). *Understanding anxious and avoidant attachments in relationships*. Lifeology Counseling. https://wefixbrains.com/resources/understanding-anxious-and-avoidant-attachments-in-relationships#:~:text=Individuals%20with%20an%20anxious%20attachment

Depierro, S. (2023, June 21). *The art of self-growth: 7 tips to nurture your inner potential*. The People Development Magazine. https://peopledevelopmentmagazine.com/2023/06/21/nurture-your-inner-potential/

Effa, C. (2022, December 6). *How to fix an anxious attachment style*. Medical News Today. https://www.medicalnewstoday.com/articles/how-to-fix-anxious-attachment-style#step-5-therapy

Emamzadeh, A. (2021, August 20). *5 reasons why some people keep sabotaging their relationships*. Psychology Today. https://www.psychologytoday.com/za/blog/finding-new-home/202108/5-reasons-why-some-people-keep-sabotaging-their-relationships

Emotional resilience. (2022, March 16). Warwick. https://warwick.ac.uk/services/wss/topics/emotional_resilience/

Eugene Therapy. (2022, August 4). *5 signs of a healthy relationship*. https://eugenetherapy.com/article/5-signs-of-a-healthy-relationship/

Fournier, A. B. (2023, March 21). *Are you sabotaging your relationships?* Verywell Mind. https://www.verywellmind.com/ are-you-sabotaging-your-relationship-4705235

Fritscher, L. (2022, November 13). *Why some people experience a fear of abandonment.* Verywell Mind. https://www.verywellmind. com/fear-of-abandonment-2671741#:~:text=In%20 relationships%2C%20people%20with%20a

Herr, A. (2015, April 18). *Building a secure attachment with your baby.* CAPPA. https://cappa.net/2015/04/18/ building-a-secure-attachment-with-baby/

Hertlein, K. (2022, March 24). *Attachment theory: The anxious attachment style.* Blueheart. https://www.blueheart.io/post/ anxious-attachment-style#:~:text=People%20with%20an%20 anxious%20attachment

Laderer, A., & Mutziger, J. (2022, February 14). *How to develop a secure attachment style so that you can have healthier, more loving relationships.* Insider. https://www.insider.com/guides/health/ sex-relationships/secure-attachment

Lewis, R. (2020, September 25). *Types of attachment: Avoidant, anxious, secure, and more.* Healthline. https://www.healthline.com/health/parenting/ types-of-attachment#secure-attachment

Madel. (2022, December 29). *10 habits of needy people and how to recognize them.* Tracking Happiness. https://www. trackinghappiness.com/needy-people/#:~:text=Neediness%20 can%20manifest%20in%20different

Manson, M. (2021, January 13). *Attachment theory.* Mark Manson. https://markmanson.net/attachment- styles#:~:text=Anxious%20Attachment%20 Style&text=They

MedCircle. (2021, February 2). *Family dynamics: Attachment theory, communication, & relationships*. MedCircle. https://medcircle. com/articles/family-dynamics/

Miller, C. W. T. (2023, July 17). 3 ways to break the cycle of unhealthy relationships and situations. *Washington Post*. https://www.washingtonpost.com/wellness/2023/06/30/ unhealthy-relationships-situations-change-strategies/

New York State. (2017, January 27). *What does a healthy relationship look like?* Welcome to the State of New York. https://www. ny.gov/teen-dating-violence-awareness-and-prevention/ what-does-healthy-relationship-look#:~:text=Healthy%20 relationships%20involve%20honesty%2C%20trust

Perry, E. (2022a, May 24). *How to know yourself: Tips for beginning your self-discovery journey*. BetterUp. https://www.betterup.com/blog/how-to-begin- self-discovery#:~:text=self%2Ddiscovery%20 is.-

Perry, E. (2022b, July 1). *What is self-discovery? 10 tips for finding yourself*. BetterUp. https://www.betterup.com/blog/what- is-self-discovery#:~:text=Self%2Ddiscovery%20also%20 involves%20trying

Ray, S. J. (2018, May 23). *5 ways to help anxious attachment and love more securely*. Therapy to Thrive! https://therapytothrive. com/2018/05/23/5-ways-to-help-anxious-attachment-and- love-more-securely/

Raypole, C. (2020, November 13). Emotional triggers: Defintion and how to manage them. *Healthline*. https://www.healthline. com/health/mental-health/emotional-triggers#finding-yours

Robinson, L., Saisan, J., Smith, M., & Segal, J. (n.d.). *Building a Secure Attachment Bond with Your Baby - HelpGuide.org*. Help Guide. https://www.helpguide.org/articles/parenting-family/building-a-secure-attachment-bond-with-your-baby. htm#:~:text=and%20your%20baby.-

Rubin, K. H., Coplan, R. J., & Bowker, J. C. (2009). Social withdrawal in childhood. *Annual Review of Psychology, 60*(1), 141–171. https://doi.org/10.1146/annurev. psych.60.110707.163642

Schuster, S. (2023, July 30). *How to tell if you have an anxious attachment style*. Health. https://www.health.com/ anxious-attachment-style-7562046

Self-esteem. (n.d.). The Children's Society. https://www. childrenssociety.org.uk/information/young-people/well-being/ resources/self-esteem#:~:text=Your%20self%20esteem%20 can%20be

7 ways to heal your childhood trauma. (2009, July 17). Casa Palmera. https://casapalmera.com/ blog/7-ways-to-heal-your-childhood-trauma/

Simpson, J. A., & Rholes, W. S. (2017). Adult attachment, stress, and romantic relationships. *Current Opinion in Psychology, 13*(13), 19–24. https://doi.org/10.1016/j.copsyc.2016.04.006

6 ways to develop a growth mindset for success. (2019, November 20). Heart-Mind Online. https://heartmindonline.org/ resources/6-ways-to-develop-a-growth-mindset-for-success

Skin-to-skin contact. (2023). UNICEF. https://www. unicef.org.uk/babyfriendly/baby-friendly-resources/ implementing-standards-resources/skin-to-skin-contact/

The Attachment Project. (n.d.). *Anxious attachment style in relationships complete guide*. Attachment Project. https:// www.attachmentproject.com/anxious-attachment- relationships/#:~:text=From%20the%20poison%20 perspective%2C%20the

UNCW. (n.d.). *Self-worth*. University of North Carolina, Wilmington. https://uncw.edu/seahawk-life/health-wellness/counseling/self-help-resources/self-worth#:~:text=Self%2Dworth%20is%20the%20internal

van IJzendoorn, M. H., Moran, G., Belsky, J., Pederson, D., Bakermans-Kranenburg, M. J., & Kneppers, K. (2000). The similarity of siblings' attachments to their mother. *Child Development, 71*(4), 1086–1098. https://doi.org/10.1111/1467-8624.00211

Young, S. N. (2008). The neurobiology of human social behaviour: An important but neglected topic. *Journal of Psychiatry & Neuroscience: JPN, 33*(5), 391–392. https://www.ncbi.nlm.nih.gov/pmc/articles/PMC2527715/

Made in the USA
Monee, IL
10 June 2024